The Best Christmas Wish Ever

Danette Fogarty

This Book is dedicated to

The joy and magic of Christmas.

May your heart be filled with faith and love.

Chapter 1

The lights of the huge Christmas tree of the Library Square Park lit up the night. It was exactly three weeks before Christmas and Sofia Randall was here, in line, waiting for her turn to see Santa. Actually, it was her niece, Chelsea, that wanted to see Santa but since Sofia was her "favorite aunt" it rested upon her to make this trip to see Santa a reality.

Chelsea, being seven years old, made most of the decisions on the outings with her aunt. Sofia didn't mind, since this was a special time for just the two of them.

The line moved slowly, but seeing the excitement on Chelsea's face as she got closer to talking with Santa, made it all worth it.

"Auntie Sofia," Chelsea asked, "Are you going to sit on Santa's lap and tell him your Christmas wish?"

Thinking for a few seconds, since Sofia wanted to use diplomacy, she answered, "I don't think so."

Looking surprised, Chelsea asked, "Why not?"

Sighing, Sofia responded, "You know, I really don't have anything I really want this year, so I'd rather give you and the other children more time with him." There, she thought to herself, hopefully that appeased her niece.

Hands on her hips, Chelsea did not look pleased. "Auntie Sofia," she said with a determined look. "Santa knows everything, so if you even have the teeniest wish," she used her fingers to demonstrate, "then he'll make it come true."

Totally uncomfortable now with her niece's lecture, Sofia looked around, trying to find something in which to distract the little girl. "Uh," she said, "look at the beautiful tree in the middle of the park." Pointing to the spot, she asked, "How do you think they got all those lights on there, especially at the top?"

Now, Chelsea sighed, "Oh, Auntie Sofia, they just used a really big ladder." She turned around to face the front of the line, apparently frustrated with her aunt's lack of knowledge.

Biting her lip, Sofia tried not to smile. She loved her niece so much, and she was finding that her niece was getting smarter by leaps and bounds. Soon enough the magic of Christmas would be a distant memory for her Chelsea. That thought made Sofia feel a little sad.

"We're almost there," Chelsea announced a few minutes later.

They were moving at a faster pace now, to which Sofia was very happy. With only three weeks until the big day, she was mentally listing all the gifts she still needed to purchase.

The elves helping Santa were smiling and asking the parents if they wanted pictures of their kids with Santa. Sofia knew she would get at least one, and give it to her brother and sister-in-law as a keepsake.

Chelsea was an only child, and only grandchild, as Sofia's parents constantly reminded her. Her brother, Grant, at least, was married and gave her parents Chelsea. He and his wife, Nicole, had been together since high school and no one was surprised when they married.

Chelsea was a gift, after a few years of Grant and Nicole having difficulty in starting their family. And since Sofia had no children, she treated Chelsea as if she were her own.

Trying to gain her niece's attention again, Sofia asked, "So what are you going to ask Santa for?"

After thinking for a minute or so, Chelsea shook her head, and answered, "I can't tell you, or it won't come true."

"Must be a pretty serious wish if you won't even tell me," Sofia commented.

Nodding, Chelsea sighed, "Auntie Sofia, some things are just meant to be between me and Santa."

Sofia tried not to laugh; Chelsea was so darn cute! Instead, she nodded herself and responded with a serious, "I understand."

They were finally next in line to see Santa, and Sofia could see Chelsea's excitement. She was hopping around and smiling at Santa's helpers.

One of the elves asked Sofia, "Merry Christmas, would you like a picture with Santa?"

After looking at Chelsea's hopeful face, Sofia nodded and picked out the package she wanted. That way she could keep one for herself and give one to her parents as well.

When the little boy in front of Chelsea was done, hopping off of Santa's lap and running to his mom, the elf guided Chelsea forward.

Standing in front of Santa, Chelsea extended her hand and said, "Hello, Santa. Merry Christmas, I'm Chelsea, but I'm sure you already knew that."

Laughing a hearty, "Ho, ho, ho!" Santa nodded and patted his knee. "I sure did, Chelsea. Come up and tell me what you'd like this Christmas."

With ladylike precision, Chelsea gingerly got up onto Santa's knee.

After posing with the elves, saying, "Say Merry Christmas!" and snapping the picture, Chelsea grew serious.

"Okay," she said to Santa, soft enough that only he could hear her, "I know that you aren't the "real" Santa, but I've been told you've got direct communication with him and I'd only like two things this year."

Not used to such precociousness, Santa tried to hold in his humor, and responded, "Okay."

"I assure you," Chelsea said with a grave face, "that I have been good this year."

Santa nodded. "Okay, then, what would you like?" he asked, ignoring the elves' persistent motions to move the girl along.

Looking over at her aunt, Chelsea winked, then turned back to Santa. "I'd like a little brother or sister but I'm not going to be picky about that," she said solemnly, "although I think a little brother might technically be more fun."

Now Santa was smiling, "And the other thing?" he asked the adorable child.

Closing her eyes for a quick second, Chelsea answered, "I'd like my Aunt Sofia to find love and get married." She pointed to her aunt, who stood patiently off to the side.

The request surprised Santa so much, that he just sat there and looked at the child. It was so unusual to have a child ask for such things in the first place, but to think of someone else before themselves, especially at her young age, really blew him away.

His answer would need to be delicate, "Well, Chelsea, I'm sure you realize that those are great wishes, but pretty big, and not really what Santa's used to hearing," he said, worried that he might offend her.

Without missing a beat, Chelsea responded, "Yes, I realize that, Santa. That's why I'm coming to you; I need some really big magic happening right now."

The pesky elves were moving in now, and Chelsea knew she only had a second or two more with Santa. She whispered, "I know you can do this, I believe in you." She hopped down and walked over to her aunt.

Sofia knew that whatever Chelsea said to Santa was very serious, given the look on his face. Just before they turned to go out of Chalet area, Sofia's eyes locked with Santa's.

It was only for a second or two, but she felt like "Santa" was looking at her closely. Smiling shyly, she gave him a little wave, then led Chelsea away.

They picked up their pictures a few minutes later and were walking around the park. There were local vendors there, mostly people who did crafts geared toward the holiday season, and a few local businesses.

Between the huge tree, the variety of decorations, and the holiday music, Sofia was feeling very festive by the time she and Chelsea left the park.

She got her niece into the back seat of her SUV, making sure she was buckled in, and then steered the vehicle slowly out of the parking lot.

Within minutes, she was pulling into her brother's driveway. The house, illuminated by Christmas lights, shone bright in the crisp, winter evening.

Before Sofia could even get out, Chelsea was out of the SUV and going up the stairs to the door.

"Mommy!" Chelsea yelled as she went inside. "I got to see Santa!"

Nicole Randall bent down so she could talk to her daughter face to face. "Really?" she asked in response, then, "And what did you ask Santa for this year?"

Shaking her head, Chelsea muttered, "Adults are really nosy," and kissed her mommy on the cheek before going to her bedroom.

Watching her daughter, a smile on her face, Nicole opened the door as Sofia was coming inside. "Boy," she said to her sister-in-law, "she's riled up."

Sofia nodded, "Oh yeah, she's not telling me what she asked for either." She hugged Nicole, and asked, "How are you?"

"Busy," Nicole answered. Her job as a nurse kept her really hopping. She really appreciated the times that Sofia was willing to take Chelsea so she could get a little more sleep.

"How's Grant?" Sofia asked, snatching a cookie off of a nearby plate. She was boggled that her sister-in-law could find time to bake between her full time job, a husband, and Chelsea, along with volunteering.

Smiling, Nicole answered, "Busy too, but we try to spend a good fifteen minutes a day together," she said dryly.

Grant was a police officer who worked days, while Nicole worked nights, so they had a tough time coordinating schedules, but, somehow, they did it.

Sofia often wondered how they managed to be so in love, with not seeing each other all that much. But, they did insist on a date night once a week that was just for them. Seeing them overcome a crazy lifestyle made Sofia hope that she could find something just as good. Maybe someday....

"Thanks for taking her," Nicole said, swiping a cookie for herself.

Smiling, Sofia offered, "It was absolutely no problem whatsoever. You know I love our "girl time" together."

Hugging Sofia again, "I know you do, and thank goodness for it." Nicole sighed.

They spoke for a few more minutes about upcoming events with their families, then Sofia went into Chelsea's room to say goodbye.

Her niece was dressed in her pajamas, appropriately decorated with Christmas trees and snowmen, while sitting on her bed with a book.

"I see you're ready for bed," Sofia said as she came into the room and sat on the bed next to her niece.

Chelsea nodded, "I am." She handed her aunt the book she was holding, "Can you read this to me?" she asked sweetly.

When Chelsea asked for anything in that sweet, little voice, Sofia couldn't resist. She knew the kid played her like a violin, and she allowed it, so why stop now. Opening the book, Sofia started reading the story to her niece.

It was a fairytale that, of course, had a happy ending in which the Prince and Princess lived happily ever after.

Sofia had just closed the book when Chelsea asked her, "Do you believe in fairy tales?"

It was important for Sofia to be honest with her niece. "You know," she started, "I actually do." Hugging Chelsea close to her, she added, "I see your mommy and daddy love each other soooooo much, that I think fairy tales do come true."

Seeming to accept her aunt's answer, Chelsea nodded, hugged her aunt back, and then slid down so she could snuggle into her bed.

Outside the room, Nicole stood by the door, listening to her daughter and her sister-in-law, tears streaming down her cheeks.

Chapter 2

Two days later, Sofia was sitting at her desk, thinking about the conversation she had with her niece about fairy tales.

Owning her own decorating business was fun, and, this time of year, it was busier than ever. Everyone wanted their house to look very merry so Sofia was usually jumping through hoops to get the houses done before the holiday parties started.

Being with Chelsea provided a welcomed break from the craziness of work. But, something about the other night was hanging in the back of Sofia's mind. She didn't know if it was the seriousness in which Chelsea was speaking to Santa, or the question about fairy tales, or even, that intense look she, herself, shared with Santa.

Feeling uncomfortable with that train of thought, Sofia tried to focus on the designs for her newest client, a woman who wanted a "Winter Wonderland to the nth degree."

Lucas Calspin walked out of his office late Monday, and was looking at his watch, frowning.

The last meeting at work ran late and now he was going to be late for his own "meeting."

His assistant, Holly, was practically running to keep up with him. "Lucas," she said, as she held out a bag for him to take, "don't forget to eat."

Smiling, Lucas took the bag, and said, "Thanks, Holly."

The poor girl, Lucas thought to himself, was probably hounded this time of year with her name being so associated with the Christmas season. No matter what, she was the best assistant he ever had so, if he heard anyone teasing her about it, they would answer to him.

He got into his car in the parking garage and turned to back out quickly.

Grabbing the bag Holly gave him, Lucas pulled out a sandwich, and was thankful for Holly's consideration. She was more like a mother to him most days, and kept him from keeling over.

Eating as he drove, Lucas made his way downtown and found a parking spot quickly.

He went into the back door of the building, finding his contact person. Her name was Leah and she was a fidgety thing, wringing her hands as he entered.

"Mr. Calspin?" Leah asked, hopefully.

Lucas nodded, and held up the trunk he held in his hand, "That's me, just show me where to change."

They walked down a hallway, with Leah saying, "I just want you to know how much we appreciate you taking on the role of Santa. Your father was always so sweet and kind, and obviously you have inherited his traits."

Getting a little embarrassed, Lucas brushed off her sentiment with, "Well, I already had the suit, so it made sense."

Leah chuckled and opened a door into a closet, where he could change. "Okay," she said. "I'll start letting the staff know you're coming and we'll see you in about fifteen minutes or so."

Lucas smiled, "Sounds good."

As Leah closed the door behind her, Lucas looked around. Never, in his whole life, did he think that he would be using a hospital triage room to change into a Santa suit so he could go entertain sick kids.

When he was a kid, Lucas always asked his mother why his father had to work so hard around Christmas. She would always have a little tear in her eye and answer, "Because your father knows what the true meaning of Christmas is."

It was years later before Lucas found out what his father was really doing during the months of November and December.

He had come across an old trunk in the attic one day, and curious, opened it up to find a beautiful Santa suit. Not one of those cheap ones you find in a store; this one was hand sewn and felt like velvet under his fingertips.

His father found him there, looking at the suit, and smiled.

William Calspin sat down, and told his son a story. He explained that when he was a child, his own father was Santa for the season in their hometown. When his father grew too ill to do it, William volunteered to take over.

He told Lucas how being Santa for little kids was very humbling. He knew that, for some children, seeing Santa was really the only form of magic they saw during the holidays. He took the job very seriously and told Lucas that he hoped to pass on that tradition to him, someday.

At the time, Lucas sort of passed off the conversation; a teenager's selfish disinterest, he supposed. But when his father was diagnosed with cancer in October, William was very afraid that he wouldn't be able to be Santa this year.

Lucas wasn't sure if it was guilt or just an overwhelming need to please his father, but he volunteered to take up the job.

So far, Lucas had to admit it was pretty cool seeing children's faces light up as he walked into the room, or a parent's smile at their child's happiness. The visits to hospitals like this were the worst and the best. He knew that these children were sick, some of them very sick, and he wanted to be the very best Santa he could be. It could be the last Christmas for some of them.

Swiping a little blusher across his cheeks to make them rosy, Lucas had to push out the emotions and focus on being jolly. It for himself, as much as it was for the kids. He grabbed the bag of gifts he brought and felt ready.

He stepped out of the room slowly, and walked down the hallway to where Leah and other staff members were gathered. They smiled as he came closer.

"Well, Santa," Leah said. "Are you ready?"

Winking at Leah, Lucas replied with a hearty, "Ho, ho, ho!"

And they were off.

Sofia came into the office the next morning, humming one of her favorite Christmas tunes. Some of the radio stations were already playing the yuletide songs twenty-four hours a day. Listening to the music helped Sofia feel more in tune with the kindness of the season.

"Good morning," Riley, Sofia's assistant, greeted her.

The thing about Riley was that she was one of the most positive people Sofia knew. And yet, even this time of year when people could be pushy, demanding, and anything but kind, Riley never wavered in her optimistic approach. Sofia really admired that about her protégé.

Handing Riley a cup, Sofia said, "Good morning, here's some hot chocolate, extra chocolate, and extra whip cream for you."

As if she had been handed a gift made of pure gold, Riley smiled brightly, and held the cup to her chest. "Thank you so much," she said to Sofia.

Chuckling, Sofia sat down at her desk.

Their office was one big room, mainly because that was all Sofia could afford. Her business was only a few years old and was doing well, just not well enough to afford a bigger place, yet.

After she checked her emails and went over her schedule, Sofia sat down at a large drafting table and tried to get an idea for decorating a repeat customer's house when she heard Riley squeal.

"What's wrong?" Sofia asked.

Tears streaming down Riley's cheeks, she answered, "Nothing, I'm just so happy." She pointed to her computer screen.

Sofia made her way over to Riley's desk and peeked over her assistant's shoulders, to see what the ruckus was about.

There was a picture on the screen, of a little girl, and Santa. It was clear that the little girl was sick, she had no hair and was in one of those hospital gowns.

"Who's this?" Sofia asked.

Wiping the tears from her eyes, Riley replied, "That's my cousin's little girl. She has leukemia, and she got to see Santa last night." Sniffling, Riley reached for a tissue, "My cousin said he was wonderful, making Brittany, her daughter, feel so special." She dabbed at more tears. "He actually brought Brittany a doll that she'd been asking for."

If Riley kept this up, Sofia would be crying within moments. She looked at the screen more closely, and commented, "Hey, I know that Santa."

There was no mistaking those intense blue eyes; she'd seen them only a few days earlier, with Chelsea.

Riley looked up at Sofia, a smile playing on her lips. "You know that Santa?" she asked her boss.

Shaking her head, "Well, I don't *know* him, but he was the Santa at the Chalet the other night, after the parade here in town."

Nodding, Riley, smiled. "Well, I think he's an angel for making little kids feel so special at Christmastime."

Sofia couldn't agree more. With a smile on her face, she went back to her drawing table and had new inspiration for her client. She made a mental note to thank Santa for his help, if she ever ran into him again.

That night, Sofia was scheduled to pick up Chelsea again. They decided to get some dinner and do some Christmas shopping.

As soon as Chelsea got into the SUV though, she seemed a little upset. In an effort to cheer her up, Sofia told her about some funny things that she had seen the last couple of days. Her niece smiled, but Sofia was pretty sure that she was faking interest.

After they pulled into the parking lot of a local diner that Chelsea proclaimed as her favorite place to eat, Sofia turned to her niece, and asked, "Okay, what's up?"

Chelsea played absently with the hem of her dress. "Nothin," she mumbled.

"Well," Sofia announced, "if you're so down, perhaps we should just go back to my house so you can relax."

The look her niece gave her was one of shock. "No way!" she said. "I'm fine," and smiled sweetly, in an effort to prove it.

Laughing, Sofia nodded, "Let's go then," she said and helped Chelsea unbuckle before getting out of the vehicle.

A few minutes later, they were seated, and ordered their meals.

Again, Sofia noticed her niece's sad face. "What's up, sweetie?" she asked her niece.

Looking unsure, Chelsea looked up at her aunt, then asked, "Do you believe in Santa?"

Very tricky question, Sofia thought to herself. The truth was always the best. "I believe that Santa represents what we're supposed to be to one another during this season: good, kind, and full of wonder."

Chelsea nodded, "Yes, but do you believe in him?" she asked again.

"Yes," Sofia answered, thinking of the blue eyed Santa she saw at the Chalet, then on Riley's computer.

Thinking for a few minutes, Chelsea perked up and replied, "Good, then I do too."

After that, it was if Chelsea's mind was lifted from whatever mental burden she had. She smiled, giggled, and told her aunt about a particular boy at school that always stole her pencil when she wasn't looking. It was such a relief to hear the daily woes of a seven year old. Certainly, it was a little easier to focus on those things than it was to worry about decorating someone's house, or bills, or decorating her own house for the holiday season.

They were finishing dinner when Sofia's phone went off. Seeing it was Nicole, Sofia answered, "Hello there, Mommy," for Chelsea's benefit.

"Hi," Nicole said, a little uneasy. "Sofia, I have a strange request for you."

Intrigued, Sofia said, "Okay, shoot!"

Smiling at one of her co-workers, Nicole tried to whisper into the phone, "I was wondering if you and Chelsea would come up to the hospital."

Chapter 3

Sofia pulled into a visitor's spot in the hospital parking lot. She looked over to Chelsea, who was humming to a Christmas song playing on the radio. Still unsure as to why they were here, Sofia helped Chelsea unbuckle and they walked inside.

Nicole gave Sofia specific instructions to meet them on the fourth floor, at room 415. It was all a little strange to Sofia, as Nicole never asked for Chelsea to come to her work, to a specific room.

They rode up in the elevator, Sofia feeling a little strange. Although she didn't have any reason to feel that way, it was like anticipation was running through her.

As soon as they stepped off the elevator, they saw Nicole, dressed in her nursing scrubs, standing at the nurse's station.

"Mommy!" Chelsea yelled, with a wide smile, and ran over to give her mother a hug.

Looking over Chelsea's shoulder, Nicole mouthed "thank you" to Sofia and motioned for her to follow them.

Nicole was walking, Chelsea holding her hand, and Sofia following closely behind, as they went into room 415.

When Sofia was inside the room, she was shocked! All over the walls were letters, obviously written by little children......to Santa.

In the bed, the patient looked like, well, he looked like Santa Claus. He was a pink-cheeked, round, man, who looked just like the persona. His beard was full and white, and, except for the IV hooked up to his arm, he seemed....jolly.

"Chelsea and Sofia," Nicole said as they crossed to the bed, "this is William Calspin, a patient of mine." She watched as Chelsea's face lit up. "He wanted to meet the both of you," Nicole added.

William, extending his hand, bellowed, "Well, hello there, Chelsea. Your mommy has told me all about you." He winked, "And she mentioned that you have been a very good girl this year."

Being seven, Chelsea stated the obvious, "You look like Santa." She tilted her head and glared at him. "Are you sure you're not Santa Claus?" she asked him.

Laughing a belly laugh that reminded Sofia of the poem, "Twas the Night Before Christmas", William shook his head, "No," then he added, "but I have direct communication with Santa."

Her eyes wide, Chelsea stepped forward and sat in the chair beside his bed. "How did you know that?" she asked him.

Smiling, William answered, "Well, you see, Santa gives all of us helpers just a little," he put his fingers up about an inch apart, "magic, so we can help him."

Chelsea nodded, thinking that made sense. "Well, then," she tested him, "do you think he'll give me what I asked for then?"

Sitting there, William thought gravely for a minute or so. "I think, Chelsea," he started, "that Santa will give you what you want."

Nicole looked over at Sofia, tears in her eyes. The look she conveyed told Sofia that this man was very sick. It was no wonder that she wanted Sofia to bring Chelsea up to see him; she knew it would lift his spirits.

William squeezed Chelsea's hand, then looked over to Sofia. "So," he looked at Chelsea, winked, and then looked back to Sofia, "what is it you would like for Christmas, Sofia?"

Stepping forward, Sofia smiled warmly and leaned over, kissing William's cheek, then whispered, "I think I'd like for you to get better."

A quick look of surprise crossed William's face, then he laughed once again. "I see, Chelsea," he looked over at the little girl, "where you get your special wishes from."

Lucas Calspin stood in the doorway of his father's hospital room, in absolute shock. He had just come from work, having a night off from his Santa duties, so he decided to visit his dad.

When he came into the room, he saw that his dad had visitors. Keeping quiet, he listened to their conversation. It took a minute or two for him to recognize the little girl and her aunt, from the other night at the Chalet.

He remembered that he told his dad about the sweet little girl who asked for a brother or sister and for her aunt to find love.

This time, he was able to see Chelsea's aunt a little clearer, and boy, was she pretty! Her chestnut hair curled loosely over her shoulders. When she leaned over and kissed his dad's cheek, Lucas felt a little put out, like he was jealous.

She whispered something that he couldn't hear, but whatever it was, it made his dad very happy.

Clearing his throat, Lucas pretended he had just arrived.

"Oh, Lucas," William said, a smile on his face, "I was just visiting with these lovely ladies." He motioned to Chelsea and Sofia.

Smiling, Lucas came forward, nodding to Nicole, then extending his hand to Chelsea first. "Nice to meet you," he said.

The little girl looked at him quizzically, as if she knew him, but couldn't place his face. He smiled, and winked.

Then he turned to greet Sofia. Now that he was closer, he noticed she had a sprinkling of freckles over her nose, and was the most beautiful woman he had ever seen. "Hi." He held out his hand. "I'm Lucas."

Feeling out of sorts, Sofia took his extended hand, and felt a rush of warmth pass through her body. "Hi," she answered, and thought her voice sounded funny. "I'm Sofia."

The two of them stood there, not sure what to do, but neither willing to let go of the other's hand.

William looked over at Chelsea, who was wearing the biggest smile, and winked at her. She winked in return, trying to stifle a giggle.

Nicole interrupted the moment by saying, "Well, then." She put her hands on Chelsea's shoulders. "We should probably get Chelsea home and ready for bed." She looked over at Sofia pointedly, "Shouldn't we, Sofia?" she asked in a loud voice.

As if being pulled out of a magical dream, Sofia rushed to the surface of reality. "Uh," she awkwardly let her hand drop from Lucas's, "Sure."

She looked over at William. "It was so nice to meet you." She smiled, then moved past Lucas.

Sofia walked out of the hospital room, with Chelsea and Nicole beside her. She felt as if she was walking on a bed of soft snow, only she wasn't one bit cold. In fact, her face felt flushed, and she wanted to laugh.

Nicole led them over to the nurse's station. She bent down and hugged Chelsea. "You be good for Auntie Sofia now," she said to her daughter.

Nodding obediently, Chelsea answered, "I will, Mommy." She looked up at her aunt, then back to her mom, "Is Mr. William really sick?"

Vowing to never lie to her daughter, Nicole nodded. "Yes he is," then added, "but you made him really happy and that does sometimes help people feel better."

Sofia noticed that her sister didn't use the words, "get better." William was simply a doll, but his son, Lucas was something altogether different. She felt like she had seen him before, but she surely would have remembered meeting a man who looked like that.

He was classically handsome, tall, dark hair, and a face that looked like it belonged on the cover of a romance novel. But his eyes, they were so blue, as if the ocean's waves transformed into them. His eyes.....

"That's it!" Sofia exclaimed, getting a look from her sister-in-law, her niece, and another nurse. "Sorry," she mumbled, took Chelsea by the hand, then mouthed, "I'll call you later," to Nicole.

Walking out of the hospital, Sofia smiled, and thought to herself, 'So that was the Santa at the Chalet, and on the internet.'

Lucas sat down in the chair next to his dad's hospital bed. "How are you feeling tonight, Pop?" he asked, using his childhood name for his dad.

"Better," William replied. "I'm going to assume that you had that little girl, Chelsea, on your lap." It was a statement, not a question.

Nodding, Lucas smiled. "She's something else," he answered.

Looking at his son, William added, "But not as interesting as her aunt, perhaps?"

His father was anything but subtle. "Pop, her aunt, according to Chelsea, wants to fall in love."

Now William laughed. "And that's such a bad thing?" he asked his son.

"Why don't we focus on you," Lucas stated, trying to defer the conversation involving Lucas's single status.

Growing serious, William said, "We are talking about me, son." He took Lucas's hand into his own and squeezed. "It would make me very happy to see you love someone as your mother and I love one another."

Smiling, Lucas retorted, "Not sure that kind of love exists anymore, Pop."

Coming into the room, Arlene Calspin asked, "What doesn't exist anymore?"

William's face beamed at the sight of his wife. Lucas always admired his parents' relationship. He had seen them fight, sure, but there was a love there that most people admired. It was hard to find that kind of "spark" between two people.

After visiting with his parents, and talking to Nicole about his dad's condition, Lucas left the hospital. He was thinking about the fascinating woman who held his hand. "Sofia," he said her name out loud. He liked that she was so kind to his father, kissing his cheek, and making him smile. The fact that, although they were virtually strangers, she made him feel comforted.

Sitting in her bed, after dropping Chelsea off with Grant, Sofia was half asleep when she swore she heard someone whisper her name.

Looking around, she realized she must have dreamt it. But then, Lucas's face filled her mind. The way his hand felt, wrapped around hers, the way his eyes sparkled like freshly fallen snow, and the way she didn't want to stop looking at him didn't leave her thoughts easily.

"Okay," she said to herself, "you sound like a stalker in the making." Punching her pillow, she laid back down and tried to sleep.

A couple of days later, Sofia was sitting at her desk when the door to her shop opened. Her eyes lit up when she realized it was Lucas, the guy who filled her dreams the last few nights.

Riley stood up first, nervously straightening her skirt. "Hello there, may I help you?"

Lucas smiled, and Sofia watched Riley's heart melt. She herself was just a victim of that magical smile the night before, so she knew how her assistant felt.

Getting up, Sofia said, "Riley, this is Lucas." She held out her hand to shake his as she walked over.

Once Lucas' hand touched hers, it was if the whole world exploded into one giant bright light. Her fingers tingled and started a wave of awareness that swept over her.

"Hello, again," Lucas responded, his smile, a little brighter, was now focused on Sofia.

Riley fidgeted. "Uh, I'll just go and get us a cup of coffee," and grabbed her purse before leaving the office quickly. It was clear that her boss and this Lucas guy were previously acquainted. Just looking at them made Riley blush.

When she heard the door close behind Riley, Sofia asked, "What are you doing here?"

Lucas smiled, "I, uh," he was a little embarrassed, "I asked Nicole where you worked."

'Note to self,' Sofia thought, 'thank Nicole.' She nodded and motioned for Lucas to join her on a sofa they used as a sitting area.

"I'm sorry to disturb you while you're working," Lucas said, feeling silly for coming here.

It seemed like such a good idea at the time. He was meeting with a client just around the corner, so he decided he would stop in to see Sofia. And the minute his eyes met hers, he was lost, in the best kind of way.

Smiling, Sofia responded, "Oh, it's not disturbing," and thought that she sounded ridiculous.

Lucas couldn't stop smiling. "I saw your sign, Home Designs in Style," he said, trying to make his pulse slow down. "So you design?"

Nodding, because she couldn't seem to find words, Sofia finally said, "Yes." She sighed. "Yes, we design homes, sometimes for when people move in and don't know how to decorate." She clasped her hands together on her lap. "This time of year, it's mostly to decorate people's houses for the holidays."

That sounded odd to Lucas. "You mean people don't decorate their own houses for Christmas?" he asked.

Sofia nodded solemnly. "You'd be surprised how finicky people are when it comes to setting their houses up with decorations."

"Well," Lucas shook his head in wonder, "I guess I could use help on occasion myself so I don't need to judge others."

His confession made Sofia chuckle. "How do you think I feel?" she asked. "My house is the worst; I'm so beat after doing other people's houses that I neglect my own."

Giving Sofia a look of mocked surprise, Lucas said dramatically, "Well, we can't have you setting a bad example now."

"No." She laughed, then asked, "Maybe you'd like to come over soon and help Chelsea and I decorate it?"

The question came out of nowhere, and Sofia was embarrassed by her boldness. She was about to apologize, when Lucas answered, "I'd love to."

Chapter 4

Two days later, exactly two weeks before Christmas, Lucas pulled up in front of Sofia's house. He noticed it looked like a gingerbread house, with scalloped wood in the gables. It wasn't huge, but not that small either. Basically, he thought it was perfectly Sofia.

They had spent an hour talking at her office the other day, chatting about themselves. Before he left, she gave him her home address and said she would make him dinner in exchange for his help with decorating.

It took them a few minutes to pick a date, each of them checking their calendars. His Santa duties kept him pretty busy in the evenings, but he had tonight open, so they set their date.

Chelsea came out of the house first, a big smile on her face. She took Lucas's hand and escorted him inside, saying, "You got Aunt Sofia to decorate, so you must be good."

Chuckling at her statement, Lucas allowed the little girl to take him inside.

Sofia's house smelled like cinnamon and spice at first. As they walked into the main room off the porch, Lucas could smell something delicious cooking. That, however, was not what caught his attention.

There was a tree in the dining room, set up in front of the big bay window. On a ladder, next to it, was Sofia. She held an angel in her hand and was reaching up to place it on the tree top.

The ladder started to wobble a little, so out of instinct, Lucas jumped into action. He was by her side in a few seconds and caught her as she lost her balance and fell into his arms.

Sofia was losing her balance a second time. The first was when the ladder tipped, but now, it was being in Lucas's arms that made her feel unsteady.

"Hello," she whispered, her face only inches from his. She could see the beginnings of stubble on his cheeks, and the spark in his deep, blue eyes that made her heart do a little flip inside her chest.

Staring into her eyes, Lucas smiled back, then managed a soft, "Hello," back.

Chelsea watched her aunt and Lucas, a silly grin on her face.

Noticing that Chelsea was watching them, Sofia tried to extricate herself from Lucas's arms as ladylike as possible. "Sorry." She tried to play off her nervousness.

After she was standing on her own feet again, Lucas whispered, "I'm not," and looked over at Chelsea to ask, "So what are my jobs here?"

Sofia stood there, watching her niece explain what they had planned for Lucas to do and tried to get her heart to slow down.

A few hours later, they were seated at the dinner table. The tree was fully decorated, and candles were put in all of the windows. Chelsea explained that the candles were put in the windows as a symbol to show Mary and Joseph that they were always welcome.

Sofia listened to her niece, and was touched by the way she took the true meaning of Christmas to heart, when so many others just focused on the gifts they hoped to receive. Some gifts, like a child understanding faith, were gifts too big to wrap;

they simply needed to be opened up in one's heart and felt.

"Dinner is delicious," Lucas said to Sofia.

She seemed quiet the last few minutes and he was genuinely interested to know what she was thinking. With Chelsea here, it probably wasn't appropriate for him to ask.

Snapping out of her thoughts, Sofia smiled. "I was just thinking how brilliant my niece is and that she must get it from her brilliant aunt."

Chelsea beamed, and nodded.

Lucas knew that wasn't what she was thinking, but for Chelsea's sake, he would accept it.

They had just finished dinner when there was a knock on the door.

Chelsea flew through the room to open it up, Sofia and Lucas following her.

"Daddy!" Chelsea yelled, and threw herself into her father's arms.

Grant Randall came inside, his smile bright for his little girl. He held her in his arms as he crossed over to hug his sister.

Sofia kissed her brother's cheek. "How was shopping?" she asked him.

Making a show of rolling his eyes, Grant told his sister, "It was like getting a root canal."

Laughing, she playfully tweaked his nose. "I'm sure it wasn't that bad," she said.

Putting Chelsea down, Grant extended his hand to Lucas. "Hi," he said. "I'm Grant, Sofia's brother."

Shaking Grant's hand, Lucas felt as if he were being inspected a little. He did know, from what Sofia told him, that Grant was a police officer. "I'm Lucas."

The men shook hands, then Chelsea grabbed her father's hand and said, "Come and look at Aunt Sofia's tree, Daddy. I helped her decorate it."

Letting his little girl lead him away, Grant smiled at Sofia and Lucas.

They followed Grant and Chelsea into the dining room to watch them and, without thinking, Lucas placed his hands on Sofia's shoulders and started rubbing them.

Sofia felt lulled into an aura of relaxation, with a sharp underbelly of awareness whizzing through her body. She smiled, and said, "Thank you."

Leaning closer, Lucas whispered into her ear, "Thank you," and kissed her cheek.

Grant and Chelsea finished inspecting the tree and turned around. Instinctively, Lucas took a step back. He certainly didn't want to get in trouble with Sofia's brother.

"Thanks again, sis," Grant said to Sofia.

Chelsea grabbed her coat and kissed her aunt goodbye. Before she turned to leave, she looked up at Lucas and said, "Thank you for helping us decorate Aunt Sofia's house and for making her smile."

Feeling humbled, Lucas nodded, and choked out, "No problem."

Grant winked at his sister, then took Chelsea's hand to leave.

Sofia, in an attempt to give both her and Lucas a little space, said, "Why don't you have a seat in the living room, and I'll open up a bottle of wine."

Lucas nodded and went into the other room. The words Chelsea said touched his heart. And, he couldn't get her Christmas wish out of his mind either.

He sat down and was thinking of the conversation he had with his father the other evening, at the hospital. His father told him that when he first saw Arlene, it was like his whole world tilted and he couldn't seem to find his footing. William also said, "If you find a woman who can do that, then she's special."

Sofia walked into the living room and saw Lucas staring at nothing. He was deep in thought. She understood because she found herself feeling the exact same way since she saw him at the Chalet a week earlier. 'Has it only been a week?' she asked herself.

"Are you alright?" Sofia asked him, as she set down their glasses of wine on the coffee table.

Lucas flushed. "Uh, yeah," he answered.

When Sofia sat down, he watched her closely. He felt himself become fascinated by the way her hair fell, in soft waves, over her shoulders. She was backlit by the fireplace so she glowed, and her smile, was so warm and inviting. He never wanted to see anything but her smile.

"Thank you for dinner," Lucas said, then picked up his wine glass and handed Sofia hers.

Tipping his glass toward hers, Lucas said, "To Christmas decorations," he toasted.

Smiling, Sofia returned with, "And to Santas who make children smile."

Their glasses clinked, sounding like a bell.

Lucas sipped the wine, already feeling drunk with being near Sofia. He tried to fight it, but found that took more effort than if he just let the feelings come over him. She was smart, independent, and cared a lot for others.

Watching Lucas over the rim of her glass, Sofia noted how nervous he looked. She felt the same way herself. Finally, she broke the silence with asking, "Are you going to tell me what Chelsea asked you for Christmas?"

A sneaky smile crossing his face, Lucas shook his head. "I cannot divulge any wishes bestowed upon me while being Santa."

His serious tone made Sofia laugh. "You're kidding, right?" she asked, expecting him to tell her what Chelsea asked for.

"Nope," Lucas replied. "It's just like a Priest taking confession. When you are Santa, you are keeping their wishes.....a very special thing."

Looking at him, so devoted to being there for Chelsea, and other children, Sofia felt herself tumbling into a feeling like nothing she had ever experienced before.

Clasping her hands together, Sofia said, "I suppose....I should let you get going. I have an early day tomorrow."

Lucas picked up on the fact that Sofia was uncomfortable, and he couldn't figure out what he had done or said to make her feel that way. "Uh, okay," he responded, and stood.

She herded him out into the entryway, handing him his jacket and saying, "Have a good night," before opening the door and all but pushing him out.

Peeking through the door, she watched as he got into his car and pulled out, before she let out a sigh. "Holy cow!" she yelled.

The next morning, Lucas arrived at work to a very happy assistant, Holly, humming Christmas carols. Working for an investment firm was not the "merriest" of jobs, but Holly seemed to have no problem keeping the holiday spirit close at hand.

He, on the other hand, could only think about a certain woman who shooed him out of her house so fast, he thought she felt he had some contagious disease or something.

Did he call her? Did he wait for her to call him?

"Earth to Lucas," Holly said with a smile, yanking him from his ongoing mental dilemma.

Blinking, Lucas asked, "Sorry, Holly, what did you say?"

Giving her boss a knowing look, Holly asked, "Who is she?"

Not wanting to give away anything, Lucas tried to play like he didn't know what she was talking about. "Who is who?" he asked her in return.

Holly placed her hands on her hips and shook her head. "My mother told me that when a man is so distracted that nothing else gets his attention, there must be a woman involved."

Of course, she was right, but Lucas didn't want to admit that he was obsessing about a designer who clearly didn't want things to progress between them.

Instead, Lucas just said, "Nope."

Letting it go….for now, Holly only nodded and handed him his stack of phone messages.

For the rest of the day, Lucas walked around in a fog. It was if his heart was left there, at Sofia's house, and he was lost without it.

At five o'clock, Holly poked her head into his office and announced, "Chalet tonight."

Nodding, Lucas finished up the email he was writing, pushed send, and then got up to get his things together.

No matter what was going on in his life, he could not, would not, let that affect how he was with the kids. This was about them!

Chapter 5

Sofia spent the day literally in a funk. She was kicking herself for not kissing Lucas the night before, and for practically booting him out of her house.

It was fear, plain and simple. He was this gorgeous guy, who did this selfless thing for kids, and his dad was sick; what could she possibly contribute to him to make his life better? In her mind, the answer was nothing.

So, instead, she came to work feeling low, and hadn't seemed to get her morale up during the day.

Riley noticed, but kept quiet. Instead, she focused on getting orders in for supplies they would need for the New Year's parties they had planned.

"Well, goodnight," Riley said as she was packing up her things for the night.

With a wave, Sofia returned, "Goodnight."

After Riley left, Sofia sat at her desk, looking at nothing. This was ridiculous! She knew it, and yet, here she was, sitting here sulking.

Grabbing her coat, Sofia decided to go out and finish her Christmas shopping. There were only a few things left, since she was such a planner, and started getting her gifts in October.

She shopped downtown, so it didn't take Sofia long to find stores that carried what she needed. She promised to get Chelsea a doll that was all the rage right now, and she wanted to get a really pretty scarf she had seen in a store window for Nicole.

During her walk, she passed the Library Park, where Santa's Chalet was. For some inexplicable reason, Sofia found herself crossing the road, heading for the park. And then, she found herself walking around the sidewalk toward where Santa sat.

She knew, somehow, that it would be Lucas there, sitting down as Santa, and talking to the children.

Trying not to look creepy, Sofia sort of stood off to the side, so she could watch him.

There he was, talking to the kids, laughing, and looking so wonderful. For an instant, Sofia considered her own mental state; lusting after a "Santa" wasn't exactly normal. But then, she reasoned with herself, it wasn't Santa she was interested in, but the man beneath the costume, but who still had the heart of Santa.

Some of the children were really nice, and others, well, they made Sofia think pretty highly of the "naughty list."

It didn't matter to Santa though; he just did what he could to make the kids happy. One of the elves announced that Santa was going to take a quick break and Sofia knew that she needed to move, or he would see her.

No sooner had the thought passed through her mind, there was Lucas, standing in front of her.

"Hello there," Lucas said. "Are you stalking me?"

Feeling silly, Sofia blushed. "I was just checking to make sure these kids weren't overwhelming you."

'If she only knew that she was the one who overwhelmed me,' Lucas thought to himself.

"I'm good," Lucas answered. "How are you?"

Sighing, Sofia admitted, "I'm feeling just awful," she started, "I basically kicked you out last night."

Nodding, Lucas waited for her to finish what she was going to say, but one of the elves stepped up to his side and said, "Santa, we need you to come on back."

Lucas turned to the elf, smiled, and nodded. Before he turned around, he took Sofia's hand, and asked, "I'm done here at 8:30. Meet me?"

She couldn't say anything, so Sofia just nodded.

After watching Lucas go back to his Chalet, Sofia went back to searching for her Christmas presents. Only now, she was smiling.

At 8:25, Sofia made her way back up to the Chalet. There were just a few stragglers left so she waited quietly until Santa was done.

Once the last child was done, he waved to her and followed the elves back behind the area where he was seated.

In just a few minutes, Lucas came out, looking like he had just come of a fashion runway in Paris, not dressing up like Santa and dealing with little kids, high on sugar, and testy.

Walking up to Sofia, Lucas smiled. She was flushed from being outside in the cold, winter air. Her eyes reflected the little light from the old fashioned street lamps that surrounded the Chalet. She was loaded down with bags.

"Hello there," he said, taking some of her bags from her in a blatant attempt to keep from kissing her.

Sofia beamed, "Thank you," and let him walk with her. "Where are you parked?" she asked. "I'm still parked down by my shop."

Lucas watched her, the wind whipping the ends of her hair up around her black, fuzzy ear muffs. She wore the look of a mischievous child ready to have a snowball fight, and Lucas found that very attractive.

He motioned toward the street. "I'll walk you to your car, then come back for mine," he said.

They started to walk down the street, lined with shops that were neatly decorated with Christmas themes. Some of the shop owners waved in greeting as they were closing up for the night.

Lucas watched Sofia greet them, or wave, and wondered how nice it would be to work in a smaller town. He worked in a larger city and, even though it was less than an hour away, it still seemed worlds different, as far as the interaction between people went.

"You like it here," Lucas said to her.

Sofia smiled, and nodded. "Yes," she answered. "I'm sure I'd do better in a bigger market," she motioned toward her shop, "but I like the small town feel of it here."

He nodded, then asked, "So what was the hurry in getting me out of your house last night?" He promised himself that he wouldn't ask, but the curiosity got the best of him tonight.

They reached her car and were putting the bags of gifts in the trunk. Sofia turned to him, and answered, "Because when I'm around you, I feel like I'm walking on clouds," she waited for a second to find the right words, "and it scares me."

Lucas shut the trunk, turned to lean up against it, and pulled Sofia into his arms. "It's Christmas," he whispered, "with magic all around us. Don't be scared." He then kissed her.

The kiss was soft and gentle, but held such warmth and trust that Sofia felt as if she had fallen into a deep pile of newly fallen snow. The softness of the landing, followed by the crunch of the packed snow beneath it, felt exhilarating and safe all at the same time.

When she could pull herself from Lucas's lips, Sofia smiled. "Well, that was a very nice gift."

She was teasing him, and Lucas loved it. "I'd like to give you that gift again, soon," he whispered.

Not wanting to get too comfortable with it, Sofia nodded and walked around to the driver's side of the car. She opened the door, allowing Lucas to hold it, and then close it behind her.

As she pulled away, waving to Lucas, Sofia was wondering if she had just opened the best

Christmas gift of all or was just opening her heart up to be broken.

The next day, Lucas took off early, in order to go and visit with his dad. The doctor usually came in to speak to the patients, and their families, in the early afternoon and he liked to hear about his dad's progress.

William's oncologist said that they caught the cancer early, which was good, but then his dad didn't respond to the treatment as quickly as his doctors would have hoped, and that's why he was admitted to the hospital.

Arriving at the hospital, he saw his mother first. She was outside his father's room, and smiled at Lucas as he walked over. "Hello, son," she said, her tone playful.

"Hello, Mom," Lucas returned. He leaned in and gave her a kiss on the cheek.

They went into William's room together, and smiled when they saw him. He was reading more letters from kids. Over the years, he sort of took on the role of reading the letters to Santa. He told Lucas it was because Santa asked him to.

When he looked up and saw his son and wife, William smiled and put the letter down. "Well, what do we have here?" he asked them.

Arlene answered first, "We were just walking around the hospital and wanted to find the best room to visit."

William smiled and hugged his wife tightly. He kissed her, and whispered something that Lucas couldn't hear, but his mother blushed at the words. Lucas was reminded of Sofia, and the night she was here visiting his dad.

"What's going on with you?" William asked his son.

Frowning, Lucas replied, "Nothing much."

It wasn't difficult to see that Lucas was preoccupied with thoughts of a young lady. Men didn't hide their feelings as well as they thought. "Is it that lovely young lady, Sofia that you're thinking about?" he asked Lucas, a twinkle in his eye.

Reluctantly, Lucas nodded. "Yes, Dad," he answered.

William took a moment to thank the Lord. One of his biggest prayers was to see his son find love. As soon as he met Sofia, then saw her and Lucas together, he knew she was the one meant for his son. The Lord truly answered his prayers.

Before Lucas could hear any more teasing from his father, the doctors came in.

Dr. Richards, William's oncologist smiled, "Well, we've finally got some good news for you today, William."

Arlene shed tears of joy, hearing that the cancerous tumors that her husband was battling, were finally shrinking. She sent up a silent prayer of thanks, and hugged her husband tightly.

Lucas closed his eyes, thankful that his father's fight was going well. He smiled at his mom, and winked at his dad. "I think that this news deserves a celebration," he said.

"Why don't you brink Sofia in to see me, and we'll all celebrate together?" William asked his son.

Shaking his head, Lucas realized his father was certainly magical in a lot of ways.

Chapter 6

Sofia was finishing up her work for the day. She had been trying to convince her latest client that putting tinsel on the outside of the house wasn't the wisest decision, when she saw Lucas come into the shop. He was smiling and his happiness was contagious.

He waved in greeting to Riley, then walked over to where Sofia stood. "Are you busy tonight?" he asked.

Pretending to think it over, she answered, "I think I can fit you in, what's up?"

"We got great news from the doctor and I promised Dad a celebration. He asked me to bring you." Suddenly, he was unsure if she would agree. "That is, if you're okay with going up to the hospital."

Happy for the good news regarding Lucas's father, Sofia nodded enthusiastically, "Of course!" she all but yelled. "But," she added, "If it's a party you want, I have some suggestions."

They sat down and started plotting.

That evening, the nurse took William out of his room for a "cruise around the hospital." While he was gone, Sofia, Lucas, and Arlene decorated his room.

It looked like Santa's workshop when they were done, and it was amazing to Lucas that she could take a hospital room and make it look so beautiful in just a few minutes.

When they were done, the three of them stood back and just looked at the room.

Arlene tried not to cry; she was so touched by Sofia's help. She knew William was very upset that he wasn't able to be Santa this year. Maybe this gesture would help lift his spirits. She asked Sofia, "Where did you get all of this?"

Smiling at Lucas's mother, Sofia answered, "Well, a few years ago, I helped with set designing for one of the school's Christmas pageants. We painted these large tapestries to look like Santa's workshop, and I couldn't just throw them away."

Lucas was in awe of Sofia's talent. "It's too cool," he said and turned around in time to see his father being rolled into the room.

When William Calspin saw what his family did for him, he was touched beyond words. It was as if he were at the North Pole, preparing gifts for children. Looking over at Sofia, he winked and put his finger to his nose.

Remembering that Santa did that in The Night Before Christmas, Sofia winked in return. "Congratulations," she said.

Holding his wife's hand, William answered, "We're not quite done fighting, but we're making progress."

Sofia thought this man was genuine in every sense of the word. It was no wonder that children trusted him, and his wife and son loved him so much. He was a man of love and faith, giving so much more, just because it was the right thing to do.

Arlene brought in a cake and smiled at her husband. "It's your favorite, red velvet." She winked at her William, "I bribed the nurses with a promise of a piece."

They all laughed and got out the paper plates and forks. After the cake was cut, and eaten, they sat there and talked mostly about Lucas's turn at being Santa. He told his father about some of the more difficult children, and then about the children that touched him with their generous wishes.

Sofia watched this family, and knew their love was strong. Her own family, although spread out, was close as well, and she felt thankful for that.

Soon after their cake was eaten, the nurses announced that it was time for William to get some rest. Lucas and Sofia said their goodbyes first and left the room so William and Arlene could have a few minutes alone.

"How does he do it?" Sofia asked Lucas as they got into the elevator.

Confused, Lucas asked her, "Do what?"

"Have so much fun and faith." Sofia offered, "He's truly an inspiration."

Thinking about it for a few minutes, Lucas finally answered, "I really think being Santa is more than just a volunteer job for him; he believes in all the magic and spirit that we should have for one another." He had to fight his emotions, "Not just this time of year, but all year long."

Sofia surely wished more people had that mindset. She promised herself to do a little better with others, since she now had such a great example. "That's a beautiful way to look at life."

Lucas walked her out to her car and settled her inside. She was a little sad that he didn't kiss her, but she figured he was probably preoccupied with thoughts of his parents. They needed him now, and that was what mattered.

William was sitting with his wife, up in his hospital room, and asked her, "Do you think they realize it yet?"

Smiling at her husband of almost 40 years, Arlene said, "I don't think so."

Nodding, he kissed his wife soundly on the mouth. "As I recall, it took me a little bit to get to that point as well."

"A little bit?" Arlene asked sarcastically, "I practically had to draw you a map!"

He laughed, knowing from the first that this woman was the one for him. "But I'm sure glad I follow directions well."

"You do, my love," Arlene said, and leaned in to give her husband one last kiss before wishing him goodnight.

Chelsea sat at the dinner table with her parents. They were discussing something about their schedules, and she was becoming impatient. Finally she said, "Excuse me, but does someone know if Aunt Sofia and Lucas are going to get married?"

The question had both Nicole and Grant fall silent. They looked at their daughter for a full minute, before Nicole asked, "Why would you ask that, sweetie?"

Realizing that she couldn't tell her parents about her wish for Santa, Chelsea just shrugged.

Grant leaned forward, "Honey, why do you think they would get married?" he asked his daughter.

Leaning her face on her palm, Chelsea mumbled, "Because they look at each other the way that Aunt Sofia said you and Mommy look at each other."

Touched by her daughter's observation, Nicole smiled, then asked, "How did Aunt Sofia say we looked at each other?"

Chelsea rolled her eyes, and wondered if her parents would ever understand anything. "She said that you looked at each other like you were the only two people in the whole wide world."

Smiling, Grant took his wife's hand, and said, "She has a point, my sweet lady."

Even now, Grant could make her blush, and Nicole hoped that never stopped. She made a note to thank him properly after they settled Chelsea down for the night.

Trying to change the subject, Grant asked Chelsea, "Are you going to tell us what you wished for this Christmas?"

Chelsea shook her head no, emphatically. "I know that Santa will make my wishes come true," she answered, but wouldn't say anything else.

After she was done eating her dinner, she asked her parents, "May I be excused?"

Nicole nodded and watched in wonder as her daughter put her plate in the sink, then kissed her daddy goodnight and went into her room.

"How did she get this big and grown up at seven years old?" she asked Grant.

Looking at his wife, "I guess she's got her daddy's smarts, and her momma's good looks," he answered and stole a kiss from his wife.

The next night was Sofia's night with Chelsea. She already planned to take her niece to see a Christmas themed movie that all the kids seemed to want to see. Personally, Sofia was partial to the TV Christmas shows that were re-run every year.

The Claymation classics would always be her favorites.

As they were clearing up the shop for the day, Sofia was trying to plan out the next week. Riley had asked for the week of Christmas off since her family was flying in from the East Coast. That meant a little more work for Sofia the week before Christmas, but nothing she couldn't handle.

That afternoon, she picked up Chelsea from school and they chatted about their day. Chelsea was still having trouble with the little boy that liked to steal her pencils. Sofia just didn't want to be the one to tell her that the little boy was probably sweet on her.

"So," Chelsea said, after they were one their way to pick up some hot cocoa at a local coffee shop, "Is Lucas coming with us?"

Sofia was surprised at the question; she hadn't considered asking Lucas for two reasons. The first being, she didn't know if he was going to have to be Santa for the evening, and the second, she wasn't sure her niece would like to add anyone to their special time together.

"Uh," Sofia asked, "I didn't ask him."

Looking disappointed at her aunt, Chelsea commented, "You know, Aunt Sofia, you can't expect a gentleman to like you if you play hard to get."

Floored by her niece's statement, Sofia didn't know if she should call her sister-in-law and ask advice, or laugh outright at Chelsea's precociousness.

She parked near the coffee shop and asked Chelsea, "Do you want Lucas to join us, Chelsea?"

The look Chelsea gave her was comical. It was filled with exasperation, "Well of course, Aunt Sofia," the seven year old answered.

They got out of the vehicle and went inside to order their hot chocolate. While they were waiting for it, Sofia called Lucas's cell phone. He answered after the first ring, and said a sweet, "Hello there."

His words melted Sofia's heart. "Hello there, yourself," she responded, then, seeing Chelsea's impatience, asked him, "I've been instructed to ask if you would like to join Chelsea and I this evening for a Christmas film at the theater here?"

Lucas would bet his last dollar that Chelsea was behind the invitation. And he would make sure to thank her, "I would love to," he answered.

Sofia gave him the information for the movie and he promised to meet them there about twenty minutes before the film started.

The ladies shared their hot chocolate, then went to the same shop Sofia went to for Nicole's scarf. There was a necklace Chelsea eyed up weeks ago for her mother's Christmas present, and Sofia promised to take her to get it. The sales lady offered to gift wrap it, so that excited Chelsea even more.

"What would you like for dinner?" Sofia asked Chelsea. She knew full well that her niece could, and usually did, say something off the wall, but she was willing to risk it.

"I'd like a hamburger," Chelsea answered.

They went to the best hamburger place in town and ate the big burgers, along with fries.

When they arrived at the theater, they saw the Lucas was already there, waiting.

Lucas had to hold back the need to kiss Sofia. He didn't want to embarrass her in front of her niece, so he took her hand instead, and squeezed it gently.

Sofia knew what he was going through; she wanted to kiss him just as badly, but they wanted to set the best example for Chelsea.

"Hello, Chelsea," Lucas said, and bowed dramatically for her.

Giggling, Chelsea returned, "Hello, Lucas." She grabbed his hand with one of hers, then offered her other to her aunt.

The three of them walked inside, hand in hand, and were determined to have a good time.

Chapter 7

When Lucas, Sofia, and Chelsea walked out of the movie, they were all smiling, and laughing about it.

"That snowman was soooo funny," Chelsea said excitedly.

Sofia felt only slightly bad that they let her have some soda, popcorn, and a little candy during the movie. Lucas insisted on paying, and made a show out of making Chelsea feel like she was the boss. Her niece ate it up, of course. Sofia realized he genuinely liked Chelsea so it was okay with her.

They were supposed to meet Nicole at the hospital so Chelsea could say goodnight, before Sofia took her home.

Driving in Sofia's SUV, with Lucas following them in his own vehicle, Chelsea asked her aunt, "So, was that a date?"

Smiling, Sofia answered, "Yes, it was."

As if she were giving her approval, Chelsea said, "I think that's a fun kind of date."

Laughing, Sofia offered, "Well, I'm glad you liked it."

A few minutes later, they were parked in the hospital parking lot.

Since Nicole wasn't assigned to the same floor that Lucas's father was on, they decided to part ways for the night in the elevator.

"Thank you, Lucas," Chelsea said. "That was a great date."

His look of surprise made Sofia laugh. "She asked," she told him, then winked.

Their floor was two so the doors opened quickly. Sofia and Chelsea got out and waved to Lucas, then turned to go find Nicole.

Lucas went up to the floor his father was on, and got off the elevator with a big smile on his face.

When he went into his father's room, Lucas smiled at the walls that looked like Santa's workshop, and the dozens of letters sitting on a table. His dad was resting, with his glasses still on.

Gently leaning over, Lucas very carefully lifted the glasses off of his father's nose and set them aside.

The sound of movement woke William up. "Hi, son," he said, his voice raspy with sleep.

"Hey, Pop," Lucas said, and sat down in the chair beside the bed. "Where's Mom?" he asked his father.

Smiling, William said, "I sent her home early tonight. The poor woman is running herself ragged and she needs rest."

For as long as he could remember, Lucas saw his father taking care of his mother, and vice versa. It wasn't just providing financially, but making sure that they each took what they needed as individuals to make their marriage that much stronger.

William sat up a little and asked, "What were you up to tonight?"

Smiling, Lucas answered, "I took Sofia and her niece Chelsea, the one you met, out to a movie."

Nodding William commented, "That was nice." Then he was nosey and asked, "Is it getting serious?"

The question wasn't complicated, but Lucas felt like the answer was. "Well," he started, "I feel things when I'm with her that I've never felt before. I kissed her the other day." He stopped, embarrassed that he was talking to his dad about this stuff.

"Go on," William prodded. "You probably don't think that your mother and I went through the same things when we were dating. Sure, things were a little different then, but the feelings of falling in love are still the same, Lucas."

Lucas knew his father was right, as usual, but it still didn't make talking about Sofia, and what was happening between them, any easier.

"You know," William shifted so he was facing his son, "I remember the first time your mom went out with me." He smiled at the memory, "I think my hands were so slick with nervous sweat that they were going to slip on the steering wheel and we'd get into an accident."

Seeing his parents as they were now, it didn't seem possible that they had doubts about their love. "What did you do?" Lucas asked him.

Sighing, William explained, "It was so bad, my nervousness, that I ended up stepping on her foot the first time we went dancing, then I spilled a glass of wine, red of course, onto the sleeve of her white sweater." He laughed, "Basically, it was all a disaster."

"And yet, she stayed with you," Lucas said.

Nodding, William said, "And she stayed with me." He touched his son's hand, "She stayed because she knew that I loved her with my whole heart." He added as a side note, "I told her that." Feeling his wife's love gave him the strength to fight now, "And I told her that I would never stop loving her."

Smiling, Lucas asked, "And you haven't?"

"Oh, there were plenty of times when I was upset, or I was the one upsetting her, but no," he punctuated with squeezing Lucas' hand, "there isn't one second that I haven't loved that woman."

As if his mother knew they were talking about her, she appeared beside Lucas. He jumped because he hadn't heard her come into the room, "Mom," he said, and stood up to give her a hug.

"Son," Arlene said back, "was your father explaining how he tricked me?" she asked Lucas.

Now, Lucas really was stumped, "Tricked you?" he asked her as she sat down in the empty seat beside his father.

William gave her a hrrmph, and offered, "Dear, I was telling our son how I told you I loved you."

Seemingly not impressed with his words, Arlene sat back and nodded, "Go on," she said to her husband.

Completely unraveled by his wife's presence, William blushed. "Well, why don't you go ahead and explain it then, my love." He smiled at his wife.

Shaking her head, but smiling, Arlene looked at their son and said, "Your father told me that we were fated to be together and that he could never love another woman."

Lucas frowned, "I may be lost here, but I don't see how that's tricking you," he said to his mother.

Arlene leaned forward, looking at her husband expectantly. When he didn't say anything, she told her son, "He failed to tell me that he was seeing two other girls at the time."

Shocked by his father acting like a "playboy," Lucas sat back and laughed. "He did?"

"Yes," Arlene said.

Feeling ganged up on, William put up his hands. "Now, here I am, sick, and you're picking on me." He tried to look pouty.

Leaning forward, Arlene kissed her husband soundly on the lips, "Yes, dear." She took his hand, "But you mustn't go spreading rumors about how you caught me."

Patting his wife's hands, William said, "Oh no, I didn't catch you, my love, you were simply a gift."

As Lucas sat there, watching his parents tease one another and love one another, he wished he had that same kind of thing.

Sofia immediately sprang to his mind. They had gotten along so well, and laughed. But, it couldn't be that easy, could it?

A while later, his mother walked out of the room with Lucas. They made their way to the elevator, saying goodnight to the nursing staff as they went.

Once in the elevator, Arlene turned to her son and said, "You know, there are no two love stories that are completely alike."

Lucas nodded, not sure what his mother was getting at.

"For your father and I, we were like peanut butter and jelly from day one." She laughed. "I always tease him about the other girls but I knew, just like he knew, that once we found one another, that was it."

The elevator door opened, and Lucas motioned for his mother to precede him. She waited in the hallway and wrapped her arm through his as they walked the rest of the way out of the hospital. "I suppose you're wondering why we're talking about this," Arlene told her son.

Looking down at his mother's face, he smiled, and said, "The thought had crossed my mind."

Arlene laughed. Lucas had gotten the best of both her and William, and she was so proud of the person he had become.

He walked his mother to her car, waited for her to unlock the door, and then helped her inside. "I know why you and Pop are telling me all of this," he said. "I just have to figure it all out."

Patting her son's cheek, Arlene answered, "Of course you do."

Lucas stood up and closed her door. He waved as she pulled out, then walked over to his own vehicle to go home.

As Arlene drove the short distance from the hospital to her home, she smiled knowingly. Men never were quite sure about love until the right woman came along.

Pulling into his own driveway, Lucas sighed. The house was dark, except for the garage light that came one automatically when he hit the button.

He waited patiently, then pulled his car into the garage. After parking, he grabbed his briefcase, and got out to go inside.

The house was quiet. He turned on lights as he went into the kitchen first, then into the living room. His house was nice; a new construction in a planned community about twenty minutes from work. He bought it because it was expected for someone like him to do so.

Opening the refrigerator, he pulled out the fixings for a sandwich, then ate standing up at the island in the middle of his kitchen. Suddenly, it seemed very lonely here.

He thought of Sofia's house. How it was warm, and welcoming, and the rooms were smaller, but somehow sweeter.

Looking around his house, he wondered if a coat of paint would make it look better. Then, he tossed out that idea and realized Sofia was what would make it better.

He picked up the phone, and dialed her number.

Sofia had just dropped off Chelsea, and was on her way home, when her phone rang. Seeing it was Lucas, she picked up and smiled, while saying, "Hello there."

Just hearing her voice made Lucas feel warmer. "I, uh," he started, suddenly not sure what he was going to say. "I, uh, wanted to know if I could make you dinner tomorrow night."

This was a pleasant surprise, Sofia thought to herself. "That would be great," she answered, then asked, "Can I bring dessert?"

"Sure," Lucas blurted out, not even knowing what he was making for dinner. Somehow, the invitation just sounded right.

Sofia laughed; he sounded so nervous. "Okay, just text me your address, and I'll come over about 6:30 if that's okay with you?"

Smiling, Lucas replied, "Sounds great."

They stayed there, on the phone for another minute before Sofia said, "Okay, then, I'll say goodnight."

"Oh, yeah," Lucas stammered, feeling stupid. "Goodnight."

After she hung up the phone, Sofia thought he was just about the cutest man she had ever met.

Chapter 8

The next day, Sofia was sitting at her desk, daydreaming, when Riley came over and waved a hand in front of her face.

"Earth to Sofia," Riley teased. "I've been trying to talk to you for about five minutes now."

Looking blank, Sofia finally returned to the present. "I'm sorry, Riley," she said. "I'm just thinking about something else right now."

A smirk on her face, Riley said, "A certain someone, you mean."

Sofia rolled her eyes, but couldn't really deny it, since it was the truth. Instead, she deterred her assistant by asking, "What did you need?"

"Well," Riley talked as she walked back to her own desk, "since this is my last day before Christmas, I wanted to know if there was anything else you needed me to do before I took off."

Trying to think, but her mind still blank, except for images of a certain Santa, Sofia shook her head no. "You go on and have a great time with your family."

Riley grabbed her coat, but stopped when she turned to look at her boss. Concerned, she asked, "Are you sure you're going to be alright by yourself next week?" She slipped her arms into the sleeves before offering, "I can probably come in, at least in the mornings."

Getting up from her desk and walking over to where Riley stood, Sofia all but pushed her out the door, saying, "You have fun with your family, I've got this."

"Merry Christmas!" Riley shouted as she made her way down the sidewalk, Sofia's laughter following her.

Going inside the shop, Sofia sat down at her desk. There was an angel Christmas ornament sitting on it, probably something left over from one of the projects they had recently completed.

Lifting up the ornament, the sun's rays shined through it and made a rainbow of color flood through. The wings glistened in the bright light, making Sofia feel warm. She decided to take the ornament over to Lucas's house so she could hang it on his tree.

Having settled that in her mind, Sofia was ready to get to work. There were a few projects in the works, for clients who wanted extravagant decorating done for New Year's Eve.

Lucas went to work, a merry Holly humming when he came in.

"How are you today, boss man?" she asked when he smiled in greeting.

Taking his messages from her, Lucas replied, "I'm really good, thanks."

Like a bloodhound on the scent, Holly's ears perked up and she followed her boss as he made his way down the hall to his office.

She watched him closely, noting a smile that didn't go away, a kind of kick in his step, and he didn't seem the least bit bothered that she was following him. Something was up. "Uh, how's the lady you're seeing?" she asked.

Without thinking, Lucas answered, "Good, thanks." Then, realizing he revealed something he shouldn't have, he turned around to see a smug looking Holly standing in the doorway to his office.

"I knew it!" she announced. Closing the door, she came into the office and sat down, preparing to hear all about the woman who made her boss so happy.

Sitting down at his desk, Lucas just smiled at his assistant. She reminded him of a child waiting for story time. "Is there something I can help you with?" he asked her.

Holly crossed her hands on her lap, looking innocent, and asked, "You're not going to tell me about the one lady who makes you look like this?"

"Like what?" he asked, clearly confused.

Her eyebrows raised, Holly shook her head, and sighed. "You look, right now, how those kids look when they see you as Santa Clause."

Now it was Lucas's turn to shake his head. "I do not. Go back to work." He pointed to the door, but was smiling, so it took the bite out of his words.

Holly shrugged, "Okay, but if you keep this up, I'm going to start calling you Santa all year."

Lucas chuckled as she left his office. Smiling, he got to work.

That evening, Lucas stood in his kitchen, and panicked. For someone who supposedly loved the holidays, he was Santa for crying out loud, his house did not reflect it.

He hadn't so much as hung one light on the outside, and he sure didn't have anything festive inside, so he was afraid that Sofia would think he was a Grinch or something.

Dinner was cooking, had been since this morning. He ran out and grabbed a roast, put it in the crockpot with potatoes and carrots, and then just planned on throwing together a salad.

The doorbell rang, and Lucas sighed. Well, it was his house, and although it wasn't decorated, he figured she would still like it.

He went to the door and opened it. There stood Sofia, loaded down with bags.

"What's this?" Lucas asked, smiling because he was so happy to see her.

Sofia handed him a couple of bags. "It's me, doing something for you," she returned.

They brought the bags inside and put them on the island in the kitchen. Sofia pulled a pie out of the first one and asked, "Do you like apple pie?"

Lucas nodded, "Oh yeah, with ice cream?" he asked her back.

Smiling, Sofia pulled out a container of ice cream out of another bag. "Of course, is there any other way to eat apple pie?" she asked him, mocking shock.

Laughing, Lucas took the ice cream from her and put it in the freezer. "Dinner will be ready whenever you are," he said, then turned around and was speechless.

Sofia was pulling Christmas decorations out of the other bags. She looked over to Lucas. "Between your appearances as Santa, and your Dad being sick, I figured you wouldn't have much time to decorate."

Touched, that she would think of him, Lucas was overcome with emotion. "I," he fumbled, "thank you."

Walking over to him, Sofia was bold. She wrapped her arms around his waist and leaned up to give him a quick kiss. When she pulled away, she asked him, "Didn't you mention something about Christmas magic?"

Holding Sofia in his arms, Lucas thought about Christmas magic in a whole new way. It wasn't just about the kids, as he always imagined it. Now, it was simply about finding what one's heart really wanted.

Trying not to make a big deal out of it, Sofia stepped away. "Now," she looked at the slow cooker, "feed me, I'm starving," she winked, "and then we'll get to decorating."

They ate a lovely dinner; Lucas set up candles in the dining room to give the room a more intimate atmosphere.

Sofia commented when they sat down, "Lucas, I think you are a bit of a romantic."

He smiled, then replied, "I'm not sure if I'm really that romantic, or you just tend to bring that out in me."

She took it for what it was, a compliment, and blushed. "We'll see, I guess."

Digging into his food, Lucas was excited about spending time with Sofia, while decorating. He couldn't remember being this excited about it since he was a kid.

Sofia insisted she help him with the dishes. So they stood at the sink, side by side, with her washing, and Lucas drying and putting the dishes away.

When the dishes were done, Sofia asked, "Are you ready for dessert?"

Lucas knew she was talking about the apple pie, but his heart was beating so fast, that he shook his head no, and asked, "Why don't we wait until we've worked up an appetite?" Now, he felt stupid for the innuendo. "I'm sorry," he mumbled.

"Don't be," Sofia retorted, "the thought has crossed my mind once or twice."

After that, Sofia went over and got her coat. She and Lucas went out to her car, where he discovered, she had a lot more stuff.

They managed to get it all inside in only two trips.

"What's all this for?" Lucas asked her, not sure where to start.

Stepping over to him, Sofia cupped his cheek, and asked him, "Do you trust me?"

Eyeing up the bags and boxes, Lucas decided it was time for a little faith. He nodded yes.

Winking at Lucas, Sofia went over to the first box. "First things first, we need to get your tree up."

Rubbing his hands together, Lucas shifted his mind into elf mode and followed her lead.

Two hours, a mound of lights, tinsel, garland, and candles later, the house looked festive.

It was clear to Lucas that Sofia was very good at her job after she helped him decorate his dad's hospital room. But now, this was a whole new level. She knew what he would need to look like he had given an effort, but it wouldn't be too much for him to take down and organize as he put it away.

Still, he wanted an excuse to be near her, so he managed to be beside her "helping" her hang things or attach garland to the stair railing. Anything to keep them close. The smell of her perfume even reminded him of floating on a cloud.

"Are you going to come back and clean this up?" he asked Sofia when they were done.

The glittering glow of candles and glittered ornaments made the room shine. Looking at Lucas, Sofia nodded, "Of course, it's all part of the service," she answered.

He led her over to the sofa, and they sat down, each of them admiring the decorated room.

Finally Lucas came out of his lull, and asked, "How about that dessert now? You've earned it."

Nodding, Sofia stood and followed him into the kitchen.

They cut the pie, heated it up a little bit, and topped it with a scoop of vanilla ice cream.

Sitting at the island in the kitchen, they each nibbled on dessert and talked about things. "How's your dad?" Sofia asked him.

Lucas nodded. "Good," he replied. "We're hoping he'll be able to be home by Christmas, but there's no guarantee."

Smiling, Sofia told him, "I'll pray for his recovery."

Her faith, so strong, surprised him. Not that he wasn't raised with it, since his parents instilled faith in him from as far back as he could remember. But, the way that Sofia seemed so sure about his father's recovery, and about everything, made him feel better.

"Thank you," he said, "and I'll pray that Chelsea gets her Christmas wishes."

Eyeing him up with a glare, Sofia asked, "Are you going to tell me what she asked for?"

Making a show of locking his lips and throwing away the key, Lucas shook his head no. "Sorry, some wishes are supposed to be a secret."

Later, when he was walking Sofia out to her car, she turned to him, and hugged him tightly.

Returning her hug was his privilege, and Lucas found it felt so right to hold her in his arms.

"I'll tell you what," he said as she looked up at him, "I'll tell you if Chelsea's wishes come true on Christmas Day, okay?"

Nodding, Sofia decided not to ask how he would be able to do that. Instead, she kissed him quickly, then got into her car.

All the way home, she sang Christmas carols until she was hoarse.

Lucas walked around his house one last time, admiring the decorations and feeling the warmth of giving. Sofia did all of this without him asking, and that made the gift all that much better.

Chapter 9

The next morning, Sofia woke up to a heavy snowfall outside of her window.

She came downstairs and sat in her dining room, her cup of coffee cupped in her hands, and watched the big, fat flakes fall onto the ground.

It was one week until Christmas and she was still determined to enjoy the holidays.

There was a tree lighting ceremony in the town square that evening. She promised to take Chelsea to it, and secretly hoped that Lucas was going to be Santa at the Chalet. She forgot to ask him the night before.

Looking at her clock, she assumed he would be at work this morning. She should be as well, but with no clients scheduled, it was more fun to take a more leisurely pace and procrastinate.

Deciding she better get a move on it, Sofia went upstairs to get ready for work.

Half an hour later, she came downstairs and heard something outside.

Frowning, she went out the back door. Her garage was detached from the house, so she knew she would have to shovel some snow. But when she went out, her back porch and the sidewalk to the garage were already cleared. Stepping off the porch, she looked to her right, down the driveway, to see a bundled up figure shoveling snow.

Pulling her hood up, Sofia walked over to where her angelic snow elf was shoveling, and said, "Good morning."

Turning around, Lucas pulled his hood back, and said, "Good morning."

Shocked, Sofia started laughing, then asked, "What are you doing here?"

Motioning to the surrounding snow, Lucas answered, "You were kind enough to help me decorate last night, so I thought it was only fair to come over today and help you shovel out your driveway."

He couldn't have made her any happier had he given her a million dollars. Sofia whooped, and threw her arms around him, hugging him tight.

"Well," Lucas said into her hair, "if I'd have known you were going to be this thankful, I'd have done this sooner."

Stepping back, Sofia beamed, "I thought you had to work."

Lucas shrugged. "I'm the boss and I work a lot, so I thought I'd take a snow day."

Her eyes sparkling, Sofia commented, "I think that's a brilliant idea."

Running back to her garage, Sofia grabbed another shovel and joined him. With both of them doing the work, they finished the driveway in about a half hour.

By then, the snow was tapering off, so they were pretty sure they wouldn't need to make another pass with the shovels.

"Come inside," Sofia told him. "You've earned a cup of coffee for your efforts."

Nodding enthusiastically, Lucas followed her inside.

They peeled off their outside clothes, hanging up everything in front of a little heater Sofia kept in the laundry room, off of the back porch.

She led the way through the kitchen, and motioned for him to sit down in the dining room, while she got out two coffee cups. "How do you like your coffee?" she asked from the kitchen.

Lucas was sitting in the dining room, looking outside, and answered, "Cream and two sugars, please."

'Funny,' Sofia thought to herself; that's just how she took her coffee too. "Good choice!" she shouted from the kitchen.

Bringing the cups into the dining room, Sofia handed his to him, put hers on the table, and then went back into the kitchen.

Curious about what she was doing, Lucas was about to follow her when she came back into the dining room. She had a basket of muffins and set them down on the table, with a plate of butter, and two knives.

"What's this?" Lucas asked her, surprised.

Smiling, Sofia told him, "I have some muffins I baked yesterday."

This woman was constantly surprising him.

"So what do you plan to do with your snow day?" Sofia asked him as they ate.

Picking out a blueberry muffin, his favorite kind, Lucas shrugged as he put butter on it, before popping a piece into his mouth.

Sofia sipped her coffee, the warmth of the fluid helped her body warm up. Of course, it could just be that Lucas was sitting across from her as well. She didn't know which it was, but didn't care. Feeling this warm and snuggly was something she would cherish.

Lucas thought for a moment, then said, "Well, I have some Christmas shopping to do…" He looked at her, a hopeful grin on his face.

'So….' Sofia thought to herself, then asked, "Is that why you shoveled my driveway?"

Feeling slightly guilty, because that was partially the truth, Lucas nodded, then rushed to say, "But not the whole reason."

Leaning forward, putting her chin on her palm, Sofia asked him, "What was the rest of the reason?"

Lucas mimicked her, and leaned closer, before saying, "The rest of the reason was so that I could be close to you."

That did it for Sofia; she smiled, and answered, "Well, you were kind…and you are cute…so, okay."

Smiling brightly, Lucas asked, "I'm cute?"

Sofia rolled her eyes. "Don't get too confident, we haven't done the shopping yet."

They got up, the sound of Lucas's laughter following them as they went out to get their coats.

Two hours later, they were at a large mall and it was brimming with people. Apparently, everyone had the exact same thought as Lucas and wanted to get their shopping done now.

"I'm sorry," Lucas said, as they stepped out of the second store they went into. "I didn't realize it would be this crazy."

Shaking her head, Sofia smiled. "I find it funny that all men seem to think that waiting until the last minute is okay, then are shocked that all the other men think the same thing."

Knowing she had him there, Lucas just smiled brightly, and tried to look innocent.

They walked along the shops casually, only going in if one of them saw something.

To be honest, Sofia was glad they were here. She had just a few gifts left, and this gave her the opportunity to get them. For Lucas, however, he seemed almost lost.

"So where's your list?" she asked him.

Pointing to his head, he answered, "Right up here."

Sofia shook her head, found the nearest vacant bench, and proceeded to sit down. "Okay," she said as she took out a pen and a piece of paper. "Who do you need gifts for?"

Looking put out, Lucas pouted. "I told you, it's in my head," he said, trying to keep the whining out of his tone.

"Without the list," Sofia spoke, "you'll forget someone, I promise you."

Lucas sighed; perhaps she was right. He did forget to pick up a gift for his coworker last year. "Fine," he answered, and started listing names.

A few minutes later, Sofia looked at him in shock. "You mean that you have to get all of these gifts and you've just started today?" She was blown away by the thought.

Shrugging, Lucas just replied, "Well, yeah."

Nodding quickly, Sofia stood up and found the nearest mall map. She started pointing at the map, then writing something next to the names on his list.

Lucas just stood there and watched. She was like a General, getting together her plan of attack. The way that she was planning Christmas shopping was probably how they won World War II. He kept quiet, though, knowing that she would help him meant more than she would know.

A couple of hours later, and half of his gift list crossed off, Lucas suggested they get some lunch.

"Why don't we take out the gifts we've already bought and put them in the car so there's less to carry around?" Sofia asked.

Since he never would have thought of something so sensible, Lucas just smiled and nodded. "I'll take them out, if you want to stand in line to order some food," he offered.

"Sounds fair," Sofia responded, her eyes scanning the food selections at the food court.

They decided on some Chinese so Sofia got in line, and Lucas made a dash for the car. The snow started up again, but it was light, and only left a light dusting on the road.

As soon as Lucas got back in the mall, his nose was assaulted with all the smells from the food court. His ears were listening to the dull roar of mall shoppers that were milling about, looking for a place to sit.

He found Sofia, because she was standing up and waving, at the center of the seating area.

Making his way over to where she was, Lucas listened to the other shoppers. Some were tired, complaining about their feet hurting, or the long lines. One lady was laughing about the gift she thought was "perfect" for her sister. Another couple was talking about whose house they were going to visit first, his parents' or hers. By the time he reached their table, he was chuckling.

Sofia looked at him, and couldn't quite peg the look he wore on his face. "Are you okay?" she asked him as he sat down.

"Yes," he answered. "I just like listening to all the things people have to say. It's funny to me what people find are problems this time of year."

Tilting her head, Sofia asked him, "What do you mean?"

He looked around, then back to Sofia. "People will complain about shopping, or whose house they'll visit first, which seems silly." Lucas noticed that Sofia nodded, then added, "But then there are people who find the "perfect" gift and are so excited to give it to the one they love."

The way he described it was comical, but sincere. "How do you feel about all of this?" she asked, sweeping her hand around to include the hustle and bustle of their surroundings.

After taking a bite of his General Tsao's chicken, Lucas said, "I like the thought of spending a snow day with a beautiful woman, and making sure that whatever I get my mother for Christmas, doesn't get me smacked."

Even though Sofia knew he was joking, there was still that underlying layer of sincerity. "Really?" she asked dryly.

"I love making kids smile," Lucas started, "and I love it when a gift I give them takes a little of the pressure off of Moms and Dads and yet, keeps the magic of Christmas alive for the kids."

That was the answer Sofia was hoping for. She sat there, at a busy mall, watching Lucas eat Chinese food, and wondered how it was possible that she got so lucky.

Chapter 10

When Sofia picked up Chelsea from school, she knew something was upsetting her niece. They drove back to Sofia's house, dropped off the purchases Sofia made at the mall, then stopped by the shop to check messages. Every time Sofia looked at her niece, Chelsea looked mad.

After stopping off at their favorite café for dinner, Sofia finally broached the subject, and asked, "Are you going to tell me what's wrong?"

Chelsea sat in the booth, picking at her food, and shrugged.

"Is it something that can't be fixed with say…some chocolate cake?" Sofia asked, and tried to get her niece to smile.

Although Chelsea's lips did twitch, it wasn't a full-fledged smile.

Having hope, Sofia continued, "Well, is it something that a piece of chocolate cake," she hesitated, then added, "and a scoop of ice cream can fix?"

Now Chelsea, even though she was trying desperately not to, was smiling.

"That's my girl," Sofia told Chelsea, and ordered them each a piece of chocolate cake with a scoop of ice cream.

When they were waiting for their dessert, Chelsea finally admitted, "I'm just upset because it doesn't seem that Santa is going to give me my Christmas wishes."

Knowing that Chelsea was quite serious about this, Sofia listened intently.

"Maybe if you told me…" Sofia told her niece, which gained her a look of 'I don't think so.'

Contemplating the situation, Sofia thought carefully. "Okay." She came up with, "How about we go and see Santa again at the Chalet and you can ask again?"

The hope in Chelsea's face was priceless. She eagerly answered, "Oh yes, thank you, Auntie Sofia."

Smiling, Sofia was glad they could solve Chelsea's problems so easily. As a child, a kindness was a life saver, and as one grew up, life just became so much more complicated.

She was thinking of her time with Lucas at the mall earlier. They had such fun, just goofing around, and looking for gifts. It was like they understood one another so easily. The truth was, though, that part of being with him was so scary to Sofia. She wasn't used to things going so easily with a man. There were steps, processes, compromises, and, in her experience, let downs. But with Lucas, it was just them being together that made everything seem okay.

"Are you ready, Auntie Sofia?" Chelsea asked, after she had finished her cake.

Coming out of her daydreams about Lucas, Sofia nodded and motioned for the bill.

They were down at the park, getting ready for the Christmas tree lighting, when Sofia saw some friends from school she hadn't seen in ages. Screaming like schoolgirls, she and her old friend, Angie, embraced. Angie had married their other friend Jim right after high school, and they had been together ever since.

Jim picked up Sofia, spun her around, and then he planted a kiss on her lips that made her laugh. His wife played jealous, but everyone knew Angie and Jim were as devoted as anyone could be.

Sofia introduced them to Chelsea, so they all stood there and chatted until the tree lighting started.

Lucas was in his Santa outfit, greeting kids, when the elves announced that Santa would take a break for the tree lighting ceremony. He got up, glad to stretch out, and then made his way toward the group of people surrounding the massive tree near the center of the park.

He just spotted Sofia when he saw a man come up to her and spin her around, then kiss her! What the…..

Overcome with jealousy that he certainly couldn't explain, Lucas turned around and went back to the Chalet.

He was still sitting there, sulking, when the elves came back to tell him the kids were lining up.

Well, even though Sofia had another guy, he wouldn't let himself get all torn up over it and spoil the kids' experience.

Chelsea stood in line and waited for Santa, while Sofia stood to the side, with Angie and Jim, talking.

Every few minutes she would look over and try to make eye contact with Lucas, but he was really busy and didn't seem to notice her.

Finally, it was Chelsea's turn to see Santa. She quietly walked up, and crawled onto his lap. "I know we've already spoken," she said solemnly, "but I don't think you understood my Christmas wishes last time."

Seeing how upset Chelsea was, concerned Lucas. "Well, Chelsea, why don't you tell me again, just so I know I didn't misunderstand you?"

Chelsea nodded. "Okay, I really want a little brother or sister, preferably a brother," she pointed to Sofia, "and then I want my aunt to fall in love."

Lucas followed Chelsea's hand and scowled at the sight of her talking with that man. Thank goodness the beard covered up his awful look.

"Looks like your aunt has already found someone," he commented to the child.

Chelsea rolled her eyes, 'adults!' she thought to herself, and 'They didn't understand anything.' She looked at Santa, very seriously, and announced, "That's not a love, that's Jim, and he knew Auntie Sofia in high school." She pointed and added, "See, that's Jim's wife, Angie."

Suddenly, Lucas felt very stupid. Sure enough, there was the Angie lady talking with them. It was plain to see that Angie and Jim were together, once Lucas re-wired his jealous brain to think straight.

"Well," Lucas said in his rough Santa voice, "maybe your aunt will find someone; she still has a week, you know."

Hugging Santa, Chelsea whispered, "There's someone she met, he took us out on a date, and he's really cool."

Wanting to help Chelsea, Santa wiggled his eyebrows, and said, "Well, that's a good sign."

"She looks all funny whenever she's thinking about him," Chelsea said, and made a funny face.

Santa asked, "And how often is that?"

Smiling, Chelsea replied, "All the time."

The elves were motioning for her to move along, so Chelsea hopped off of Santa's lap and waved goodbye.

Sofia walked over and took her hand, raising a hand to wave to Santa herself.

There was never a time, before now, that Lucas wanted to take off his suit during his appearances. He so badly wanted to go with Sofia and Chelsea to do whatever they wanted to do.

The next child came up, and was shy, so Lucas turned his attention to her. He wanted all the kids to feel welcome by Santa. When he looked up again, Sofia was gone.

With only six days left until Christmas, Sofia figured she had better get started on her holiday baking. Donning her apron, the one with little snowmen on it that was reserved strictly for making Christmas goodies, she waited for her sous chef to arrive.

Grant brought Chelsea over to Sofia's house. He pulled in the driveway, noting that it was expertly shoveled, and knowing that his sister, with her many talents, hadn't done that.

"Hey," he said to Sofia when he and Chelsea came inside. "Did you finally hire someone to shovel the drive?" he asked her, while slyly searching for something sweet to nibble on.

Handing her brother a store bought Christmas cookie, Sofia shook her head. "No, actually, Lucas came over yesterday morning and did it for me."

Taking note of the information, Grant only nodded. His wife would need to know about this when he saw her later.

Looking at Chelsea, Sofia asked, "Are you ready to be responsible for some of the most delicious things we eat on Christmas Eve and Christmas Day?"

With a serious look, Chelsea smiled and nodded, before saying, "Daddy says that your cookies are better than Mommy's." She leaned in and whispered, "But we're not supposed to tell that to Mommy."

Grant only shook his head, then bowed out, with plans to do his own last minute Christmas list, courtesy of his wife.

When they were left alone, Chelsea went into the living room and turned on the radio. She found the station that was playing Christmas music, and cranked up the volume.

Sofia pulled out a step stool, so Chelsea would be at counter height with her, and started pulling out ingredients.

The agenda was to make five different kinds of Christmas cookies, some mini cakes, and some homemade breads. Sofia made up plates for her neighbors, some of their relatives, and a few friends. She delivered them on the 23rd as sort of her own Christmas tradition.

Baking would take up almost the entire day, then she would spend the next couple of days wrapping the plates up festively. Any extras would be taken over to a homeless shelter in a nearby town but, of course, there were a few left over for Chelsea and Sofia to sample.

"Let's get going," Chelsea announced, and they got to work.

Hours later, they were both smeared with flour, but giggling at the mess they made in the kitchen. The cooling racks covered the dining room table from end to end, and were starting to fill up with goodies.

They were rolling out the dough for sugar cookies when Chelsea turned to her aunt and asked, "Are you in love?"

The question threw Sofia a little, since it was out of the blue, and mainly, since she had been pondering it herself over the last two weeks. Since meeting Lucas, nothing seemed the same. She wondered if it was simply the spirit of the holidays that made it seem so exciting, but she wasn't sure.

Seeing that her niece required an answer, Sofia said, "Well, falling in love is a lot like making cookies, you know."

Chelsea looked skeptical, and asked, "It is?"

"Sure," Sofia replied. "First, you need to have the right ingredients, right?" she asked her niece.

Dutifully nodding, Chelsea said, "Or it doesn't turn out right."

Nodding in return, Sofia replied, "Exactly."

Not to be deterred, Chelsea asked her, "So, do you and Lucas have the right ingredients?"

Smiling down at her niece, Sofia answered, "I think we've got them, but it takes a while to know." She pointed at the oven. "Just like it takes time for the cookies to bake, it's not an instant kind of thing."

As if she were contemplating her aunt's answer, Chelsea was quiet for a long while. Sofia was wondering if her niece believed her, and was worried that she was somehow mentally screwing her up, since she didn't answer the right way.

Finally, Chelsea looked at her aunt and announced, "Well, I see you look at Lucas and him look at you like Mommy and Daddy look at each other." She helped Sofia pull out the next pan of cookies, then added, "And you've told me that Mommy and Daddy are in love, so you must be too."

Sofia laughed. Chelsea had such an easy way of putting everything out so clearly. If adults were as open and honest as children were, Sofia was pretty sure the world would be a much better place.

The girls were just about done with their baking, when there was a knock on the door.

Grant came back in, making a production out of sniffing the air. "Oh, I think there are some Christmas cookies in here with my name on them," he announced.

Chelsea laughed at her father, and proudly produced a sealed sandwich bag with a few cookies already inside. "These are for you." She gave the bag to her father. "Aunt Sofia says that if we don't bribe you right away, you try to eat up all of our efforts."

Laughing, Grant winked at his daughter and said, "Your aunt is one smart cookie!"

The pun had Chelsea breaking out into giggles, and Sofia shaking her head in exasperation.

Chapter 11

It was five days until Christmas, and Sofia awoke with purpose. Today was going to be a day spent cleaning the house and wrapping gifts. To others, that may have seemed like a couple of menial tasks, but Sofia loved showing off her house for the family Christmas party, and she absolutely loved wrapping gifts.

As she rushed around from room to room, dusting, sweeping, mopping, or rearranging, she thought about her life. It was full, it was happy, and she felt successful with her business…..but.

That but was a very big one, because it included Lucas. When she was with him, none of those other things changed; it was as if she felt more complete with him there.

Another but was, that they had only shared a few kisses, not that she was rushing things, but it did open up their relationship to interpretation. She had never asked him about it, if he thought they were dating, or if he even was up for any kind of relationship.

Come to think of it, they really only discussed the very surfaces of their lives.

She was finishing up the last room, when her cell phone went off. Seeing it was the object of her thoughts, she picked up, a smile on her face, and said, "Hello."

Lucas had just ended his stint as Santa, and he was tired and hungry. He changed out of his suit and called Sofia first thing, not worrying about the other things he needed. "Hello yourself," he said, then asked, "What are you up to today?"

Sitting on the stairs, Sofia answered, "I just finished cleaning my house, and I'm about to start wrapping gifts."

Amazed at her organizational skills, Lucas sighed. "Oh yeah, now that I bought things, I guess I'll have to wrap them." His tone was less than thrilled.

Sofia laughed at the sound of his voice. He sounded like a little boy, who had just been told what chores to do. "I'll tell you what," she said, "If you pick up some sandwiches from my very favorite place, I'll help you wrap your presents."

The deal sounded too good to be true, so Lucas pounced, with a resounding, "Sure!"

They discussed the deli that Sofia raved about, and she gave him her order. He told her he would be there in about half an hour and they hung up.

Running around, Sofia decided that she needed to change clothes. Her cleaning attire was certainly not acceptable for any guests to see, much less the most handsome man she had ever laid eyes on.

After running around, putting on a little mascara and blush, pinning her hair back so it looked decent, and making sure she had on her best perfume, she felt presentable.

The doorbell rang and she ran downstairs, almost falling as she went.

By the time she answered the door, her cheeks were flushed from the rush of adrenaline, and seeing Lucas again.

"Hi," she said, almost shyly.

Lucas smiled in return. Lord, the woman was beautiful. Her long brown hair caught the rays of sunlight that came through the doorway, making it look as if it glowed. Her eyes, green as a spring meadow, sparkled. All he could get out was, "I brought lunch," and walked in, as Sofia stepped aside.

They ate lunch at the dining room table, Sofia regaling him with stories of her experiences eating at the deli, as a kid. He laughed at her antics and, even though he was hungry before, he seemed to lack his appetite now.

Sofia noticed that he barely touched his sandwich. "Aren't you hungry?" she asked, afraid that he didn't like the food.

"Yes," Lucas replied, then took a bite to prove it. "I guess I was just caught up in our conversation."

Smiling, Sofia nodded. "I've done that a time or two, myself," she told him, before standing up.

She left the room but came right back in, with a heaping plate of cookies. "Here are some of the things Chelsea and I made yesterday."

Selecting two cookies, so he didn't appear to be a glutton, Lucas put them aside until he finished his sandwich.

Sofia cleaned up their wrappers, then left again. When she came back this time, she was carrying a very large, plastic tote.

"Dare I ask?" Lucas inquired.

Smiling slyly, Sofia replied, "These are all the necessary supplies to wrap Christmas presents like a pro."

A little intimidated, Lucas's smile fell. "A pro?" he asked.

Bending down to open the container, Sofia assure him, "Don't worry, I'll be here to show you how to do it."

Still unsure, Lucas nodded.

After he finished his sandwich, Sofia asked him to go out to his car and get the gifts he purchased.

When he came back in, she was seated on the floor in the living room, wrapping paper arranged on one side of her, and scissors and tape on the other.

His little pile of presents didn't seem so little now that they had them all together in Sofia's living room. Even she looked a little surprised at the sheer number of gifts.

"Do I need to go and get some more wrapping paper?" he asked her, sitting down on the floor beside her.

Sofia shook her head no. "I don't think so," she answered. "I've got more in another container if this isn't enough."

Again, Lucas was amazed. "How do you keep this all straight?" he asked, trying to decide which paper he wanted to use for his assistant, Holly's, gift.

Laughing, Sofia replied, "It's not really keeping it straight for me, it's just fun."

"It's more like a nightmare," Lucas mumbled. He smiled when Sofia laughed outright at that.

She smiled when he picked up a particularly festive paper, and said, "Good, you've chosen your paper. That's really the hardest part."

Looking at her worriedly, Lucas asked, "Should I be concerned about what type of wrapping paper I choose?" He usually just picked up some stuff on sale and asked the people who wrapped outside the stores to do it, or roped his mother, or Holly, into it.

Considering his question, Sofia offered, "I kind of look at wrapping paper as a reflection of the person giving the gift, and of the person receiving the gift." She picked up the doll she found for Chelsea and grabbed a roll with little reindeer on it. "You see, this represents fun and frolicking, and that's how I see Chelsea."

"Did you just use the word frolicking?" Lucas asked, trying not to laugh.

Rolling her eyes, but laughing with him, Sofia retorted, "Yes, but its appropriate wording for this time of year."

Lucas saluted her, and focused on his gift. "Okay, we've got the paper, now what?" he asked.

For the next hour, Sofia showed him, repeatedly, how to wrap presents. She had to admit, he wasn't half bad, but his first few gifts did kind of look like something Chelsea would wrap, if given the supplies. But, not wanting him to feel bad, she encouraged him to go slowly and enjoy the event.

After about the tenth gift, Lucas was tired. He looked over and still saw a pretty good sized pile of gifts. Thank goodness nothing he bought was big. He watched Sofia wrap a large toy for Chelsea, and a very soft looking blanket for a friend. He was pretty sure he would've given up at that point and just tossed it in a bag.

"You are really good at this," he said to her, smiling.

Looking over at Lucas, a twinkle in her eye, Sofia asked, "Is that your way of flattering me into doing some more of your wrapping?"

Lucas faked considering her question, then said, "Well, I sure wouldn't mind it, but I think I can make it through if I get a few more cookies."

Sofia shooed him out of the room, and continued wrapping her own gifts.

Lucas walked into the dining room, and grabbed a few more cookies. He stood there, watching Sofia, Christmas music in the background, the smell of cookies in the air, and thought that there was nowhere else he would rather be at this moment.

When Sofia looked up, she saw Lucas watching her intensely. His gaze made her feel a little vulnerable, but warm in a good way as well. She wondered if he was thinking all the things she had been thinking, but decided now wasn't the time to bring it up.

"You'd better get over here and finish your wrapping," she said to him in a motherly tone.

Grabbing one last cookie, Lucas nodded, and answered, "Yes, ma'am," before joining her in the living room once again.

A few more hours passed and the wrapping was done.

There was a pretty large pile under Sofia's tree, and his presents were all safely tucked back into his trunk.

They were now sitting on the sofa, contemplating whether they should open a bottle of wine.

"I really want to," Lucas said, looking at his watch, "but I promised Dad I'd go up and see him tonight since I'm off of Santa duty."

Nodding in understanding, Sofia smiled, then asked, "How is he?"

Now it was Lucas's turn to smile. "Doing better every day. He's now complaining about going home."

"That's good," Sofia said, opting to grab them each a bottled water.

When she came back, he nodded in thanks, then offered, "I'm not sure if my mom is glad he's complaining, because that means he's getting better, or trying to get her annoyed."

Chuckling, Sofia responded with, "Probably a little of both."

Knowing that he had to leave at some point, and not wanting to, Lucas tried to keep the conversation light. He asked Sofia, "So what are your plans these last couple of days before the big night?"

That was a bigger question than he thought, because Sofia had to reach over and grab her planner before she answered. "Well," she started, "tomorrow we have a block party of sorts; all the shop owners get together for a little food and drink," she winked, "to kind of give ourselves a little boost before the big sales push." Sofia pointed to a big box that was wrapped. "That's my white elephant gift for that.

"Then, the next day, I'm taking Chelsea ice skating, then we're going to the mall so she can get some presents for her parents." At Lucas' horrific face, she said, "I know, right, it will be sheer chaos."

She glanced at her planner and said, "On the 22nd, there's a group of us who Christmas carol for some of the retirement homes in the community." She laughed at Lucas's skeptical look. "It's really is fun, and it's nice to visit with people who might not otherwise get visitors for the holidays."

Watching Sofia, and seeing how much she thought about others, made Lucas want to be around her even more. He leaned in, and kissed her softly.

Lucas's lips on hers made her insides melt, and Sofia sighed as he pulled them away. "What was that for?" she asked, then felt silly.

Smiling, Lucas answered, "It was for you being you."

That's when Sofia knew she had fallen…headlong, without a doubt, into love.

Chapter 12

The next couple of days flew by. With parties and plans, Sofia kept herself busy. But even with all of that, she was still feeling lonely. Lucas had appearances as Santa scheduled, and she completely understood, but was also completely sad that they couldn't see one another.

On the morning of the 23rd, Sofia got up with a purpose. She was delivering her goodie plates today and visiting with friends she didn't get to see often.

Funny how life just sort of filled up your days, and you forget how much other people meant to you. Surely most people were guilty of that from time to time, but at this time of year, Sofia put forth the extra effort to make sure everyone she held dear, knew it.

After bundling up, Sofia visited her neighbors first.

One of them was an elderly couple who delighted in regaling Sofia about their grandchildren's adventures. They all spoke about local events and even touched on the increases in the local property taxes. It wasn't what was said, as much as it was the time taken to spend with friends.

Her other neighbor had a houseful of kids, and had additional family visiting for the holidays, so Sofia didn't stay long. They did thank her profusely for the food, as the kids started scarfing it down almost as soon as Sofia put the plate down on the table. With merry wishes, Sofia said goodbye a short time later, and went home.

Grabbing the rest of her plates and making sure they were labeled, Sofia put them in the back of her SUV, and took off to deliver them.

She visited with a great-aunt, who she would see in a few days, but wanted to check on anyway.

Friends from school were given plates, and they all caught up on the goings on in the recent year.

By the afternoon, Sofia was famished, so she stopped off at her favorite deli, the one Lucas got their lunch from just a couple of days before. She was ordering a sandwich when her phone went off.

"Hello," she said quickly, hoping to get whoever was on the line off of it before she went up to order.

Lucas smiled warmly, and said, "Hello there, delivery girl."

Surprised by his greeting, Sofia looked around. "How did you know I was doing that?"

Chuckling, he shuffled papers on his desk. "Because you told me the other day, after we did our instructional wrapping."

Remembering, she felt silly. "Oh, sorry," she mumbled.

"Are you okay?" Lucas asked. Her voice sounded a little off.

Torn, Sofia wasn't sure whether she should be honest, or just play it off. Well, life was a gamble, or so she had been told, so now was not the time to show her cards. She sighed, then answered him with, "Well, I've been missing you." She rushed to cover up her silliness, "It's just that we've been spending so much time together, and we've been having fun."

Thinking that Sofia was sweet, Lucas decided to be up front with her as well, "Why do you think I'm calling you, sweet lady?" he asked, then said, "I thought that just hearing your voice would make my day better and it did."

It was words like that from Lucas, that made Sofia's heart just melt. "Really?" she asked, insecure that it was only her who felt this way.

"Really," Lucas responded. "How about," he started to say, but stopped to answer a question Holly had for him quickly. After his assistant left, he said into the phone, "we meet for a late dinner tonight?"

Smiling widely, Sofia nodded, then realized he couldn't see her, so she said, "Yes," a little breathlessly.

He should be honest with her. "I'm going up to the hospital to see Dad, and, although I know this is certainly not the best way to have dinner, I was hoping we could meet in the hospital, visit with Dad, then go get some food at the cafeteria."

Standing there in a deli, with dozens of people rushing around her, Sofia couldn't think of a better invitation. She responded, "Yes!"

After her phone call with Lucas, Sofia's mood improved tenfold. Just knowing she would be seeing him made her giddy. It was crazy, sure, but life wasn't supposed to be boring or predictable. She dropped off the rest of her plates, visiting pleasantly, then went to pick up Chelsea at her school.

She was at the school, waiting for Chelsea to get out, when she realized she should have made a plate of goodies for Lucas's parents, and the nursing staff at the hospital.

When Chelsea got in the car, Sofia asked her, "How do you feel about a little last minute baking?"

Smiling, her niece answered, "Sure, I don't have any homework for the holiday break."

They went back to Sofia's and started putting together a few more plates. One of them was huge, since Sofia knew there were a lot of nurses on staff up at the hospital.

At 6 o'clock, they bundled up and left the house, plates in tow.

As soon as Sofia made the change in plans, she called Grant to see if he could meet her at the hospital to pick up Chelsea.

They pulled into the parking lot, and went inside. Chelsea insisted on carrying the much larger plate, and almost dropped it a few times. Sofia tried to be supportive but kept her hand on Chelsea's shoulder, just in case.

Grant met them on the second floor, since that's where Nicole was assigned to today.

The two cookie makers got off the elevator and went straight over to the nurse's station. Since most of the nursing staff knew Chelsea, they came over and greeted the little girl warmly.

"We brought cookies!" Chelsea announced, and got a round of applause.

Sofia just stood back and allowed her niece to bask in the limelight for a few minutes. Her sister-in-law came up behind her and whispered, "That child is so spoiled."

Turning around, Sofia hugged Nicole, then answered, "But she's spoiled in such a good way."

Nicole laughed and went over to her daughter, to give her a hug.

Checking her phone, Sofia knew that she had to go so she could meet Lucas on the fourth floor, then have dinner.

As if sensing her sister-in-law's anxiousness, Nicole told her, "You go on. We'll keep an eye on her until Grant gets here; he just texted and said he's on his way."

Sofia didn't wait for any further prompting, and with a wave, she got back onto the elevator.

After pushing the button for the fourth floor, she stood there with a plate of cookies, feeling really nervous.

"This is crazy," she mumbled to herself. She loved him, that was fine, but it didn't mean he loved her back and it sure didn't mean that she had to act like an idiot when she was going to see him.

As the elevator door opened up on the fourth floor, Sofia felt strong. She stepped off, turned toward the right, saw Lucas, and her whole being melted into a big pile of gooey love.

'Darn it,' she reprimanded herself, 'keep it together.'

Lucas saw Sofia and smiled brightly. Seeing her was the highlight of his day.

They met up halfway down the hallway, both smiling big, but not really knowing what to do. It was awkward, but in a sweet way.

"Uh," Lucas started to say, "Mom and Dad are both here, so why don't we go in?"

Nodding, Sofia followed him into his father's hospital room.

Arlene Calspin stood up and came over to greet them. "Lucas and Sofia, thanks for coming up."

Smiling at Lucas's mother, Sofia handed her the plate. "I made a plate of goodies; I thought you could use them."

Giving Sofia a quick hug, Arlene took the plate and set it on a table in the corner. "As soon as this one comes home, he can have some," she said, pointing at William.

William looked determined when looking at his wife, but the twinkle never left his eyes. Then he turned to Sofia and smiled widely, "Sofia," he said, and patted the vacant seat beside him. "Come, sit."

Sofia did as she was asked and sat down. William asked her about her holiday plans so she filled him in on the last couple of days' festivities.

"What do you do on Christmas Eve?" William asked, when she was done.

Taking a deep breath, Sofia answered, "Well, we do some Christmas caroling in my brother's neighborhood, drink egg nog, a lot if possible," she winked when William laughed, "Then my father always reads the Christmas Story to us." She amended, "Well, really to Chelsea now, but he read it to my brother and I when we were younger."

"That's sweet," Arlene said.

Nodding, Sofia agreed. "We think so; it's important to stand with tradition."

Now William nodded, "I couldn't agree more."

Looking at Lucas, Sofia asked, "What do you do?"

"Well," Lucas smiled at his parents, "we will make a big dinner, then Dad would go out and surprise some special kids for an hour or two. Mom and I would go along so we could be together as a family, then we would come home and collapse." He made it look dramatic by flopping his hands and head down.

They all laughed.

"I'll bet you were exhausted," Sofia directed to William.

Shaking his head no, he replied, "I never felt exhausted. I guess I always felt like it was a privilege so it actually gave me energy." He looked at his son, "Now it's Lucas's turn, if he chooses to continue it."

His statement surprised Sofia. She guessed that William would take up his role as Santa as soon as he was better. She wondered if Lucas, given the choice now, would continue the tradition.

The four of them spoke for a little longer, with Lucas's parents thanking Sofia once again for the cookies.

Leaving the room, Lucas's hand on her back to guide her, Sofia felt a whole new kind of warmth. It spread from her heart to the tips of her fingers and toes.

They got some food from the cafeteria, opting for some pre-made sandwiches as opposed to the hot dishes. The sandwiches seemed like the safer bet, and they laughed about hospital food.

During their dinner, Lucas stayed quiet, content to allow Sofia to tell him about her day. Tomorrow was Christmas Eve and he would be going to the hospital near where he lived to spend a few hours with the very sick kids. He looked forward to it, and dreaded it at the same time. Sending up a prayer, he hoped that the children he was seeing were not celebrating their very last Christmas.

"You're quiet," Sofia commented. She had been rambling on, and knew he was listening, but then his eyes lost their shine.

Smiling, Lucas responded, "I was just thinking about tomorrow, and my visit with the kids." He took her hand into his. "They're very sick, and I hope it's not their last Christmas."

Such heavy thoughts from such a caring man. Sofia wasn't sure it was possible, but she fell deeper in love with him.

"After we first "met" when I took Chelsea to the Chalet," Sofia told him, "my assistant pulled up a picture of you, on Facebook, with her sick cousin." Tilting her head, she studied Lucas's face. "I can't tell you how happy that child's face made Riley, and her little cousin's mom." Squeezing Lucas' hand, Sofia said, "You should be proud of what you do."

Hearing the words from Sofia helped Lucas make the big decision he had been dreading since he took this up....would he continue being Santa?

Chapter 13

Christmas Eve morning, Sofia was up early. She was picking her parents up from the airport, then taking them over to Grant and Nicole's house.

Their parents moved to Phoenix, since they enjoyed the milder, dryer weather. But, every Christmas, they flew home to be with both her and Grant. Ever since Chelsea was born, things were even better, and their parents trying to make the most of the time with their granddaughter.

Sofia waited in the cell phone lot at the airport. Her father insisted that she not spend money on parking, when they could just call her and have her swing by to pick them up.

Pulling up to the curb about half an hour later, Sofia was all smiles. "Welcome home." She greeted her parents, then helped them put their bags in the back of the vehicle.

They chatted about all sorts of things, on their way to Grant and Nicole's house. It was fine until her mother asked, "So are you seeing anyone?"

The way her mother asked the question meant that either Grant or Nicole spilled the beans about

Lucas, and she had to come clean. She plotted her revenge against them in her head. "Uh," she looked over at her mom, "yes, I've been seeing a very nice man."

Her father leaned forward, so he was in between the front seats, "Are we going to meet him?" he asked Sofia.

Feeling the pressure, Sofia just smiled benignly. "I'll ask him," she answered.

Sofia was relieved when they arrived at her brother's house. Then her parents would dote on Chelsea and not hound her about her love life.

They all went inside, greetings exchanged, and then Grant and their dad went out to bring in the bags. Seeing the opportunity to get information, Sofia pulled Nicole aside and whispered, "Okay, who blabbed about Lucas to Mom and Dad?"

Smiling, Nicole pointed to her daughter, and answered, "There's your culprit."

Okay, so she really couldn't get mad at a seven year old, but still, this could be really uncomfortable. She had never asked Lucas to come over, which now, she realized was totally stupid.

The guys came back inside and she had to push aside her thoughts and focus on her family.

Lucas was smiling, like a little kid, as he drove his parents home from the hospital. His father's doctor gave him the thumbs up just this morning, and they were out of there before the ink dried on the medical orders.

William was still very weak, but he was able to get inside, under his own power, and Arlene guided him to his easy chair in the living room.

"I never thought I'd be happy to be wearing pants and a belt," William commented, prompting a giggle out of his wife. "I'll just sit here for a bit and watch TV, if that's okay."

Arlene smiled. She didn't care if her husband only wanted to sit in that old chair; he was home, and on the mend.

She walked into the kitchen, followed by Lucas, and started making some coffee. "Thank you for driving us home," she told her son. "I was afraid I wouldn't be able to handle him."

"No problem, Mom," Lucas responded, and kissed her on the cheek. "I'll come by later, after my trip to the hospital and we'll spend Christmas here, together."

Cupping her son's cheek, Arlene's eyes filled with tears. "I cannot think of a better thing to do." She turned back to the coffee maker. "Except," she pointed out, "maybe if Sofia were to join us."

Lucas rolled his eyes, "I didn't ask her, Mom, plus, she has plans with her own family."

Knowing her son, Arlene knew that he was just as disappointed to be without Sofia, but he probably wouldn't admit it. "That's fine," she said, and looked in on her sleeping husband.

Sofia helped Nicole make a big turkey for Christmas Eve dinner. Her mother's and father's siblings came by during the evening to say hi, nibble on some food, then go on to their own family's houses. It was fun seeing everyone, but Sofia still found herself checking the clock, or her phone, to see the time and wonder what Lucas was up to.

At 7pm, a group of friends met up at the house, and everyone prepped for their traditional Christmas caroling. The house was filled with laughter, and everyone practiced the songs, halfheartedly of course, but still, it helped.

They bundled up, and everyone went out, going down the street, and stopping at their regular houses to sing a few songs.

Lucas arrived at his parents' house, and smiled. His mother had obviously been cooking dinner, and he was glad. The time with the kids was great, him giving out gifts and seeing their faces light up, was just amazing.

"How did it go?" his mother asked him, as he took off his jacket.

Lucas smiled. "Great." He gave her a hug. "I now know why Dad insisted on doing it all these years."

Nodding, Arlene offered, "I'll bet you thought he wanted to be out more than he wanted to be with us, didn't you?"

The question was one he had asked as a child, so he nodded his head yes.

They sat down at the table, after Arlene peeked in on William, just to make sure he was okay. She held her son's hand as she explained, "It was never that he wanted to be away from us, Lucas." She tried to hold back the tears. "It was that he knew how lucky he was to have us, healthy and happy."

The new perspective Lucas gained this year humbled him. "I'm figuring that out," he said to his mom. He started twisting his hands together and asked, "Can I ask you a favor?"

Smiling, Arlene said, "Anything."

The group of carolers were making their way down the street. They started with the simple carols like, We Wish You a Merry Christmas, and Jingle Bells.

A couple of blocks over, the group stopped.

Sofia looked at Nicole, and asked, "What's wrong?"

Pointing at the next house, Nicole answered, "We've never stopped at that house, because the lights were always out on Christmas Eve."

Her eyebrows raised, Sofia answered, "Well, it seems like somebody's home tonight, so we should stop."

The group agreed so they all gathered on the front stoop, and started in with "Silent Night…..Holy Night…."

Arlene was doing the dishes in the kitchen when she heard the doorbell ring. Wiping her hands on the towel, she went to the door and opened it. There stood a group of people singing Silent Night. She was touched by their song. As soon as she realized who was singing, Arlene called out to her son, "Lucas, can you come here please."

Lucas heard the singing as he came to the front door. He smiled, then stopped when he saw Sofia was one of the carolers. How did she know where his parents lived?

Sofia was singing loudly, when she felt Chelsea pull her sleeve. Looking up, Sofia saw Chelsea pointing to the doorway of the house. She lifted her eyes, and they saw Lucas and his mother standing there, looking as surprised to see her as she was to see them.

Lucas watched her as she sang, the group sounding really good.

"Jesus Lord, at thy birth," they sang, and quieted down.

Stepping forward, Sofia walked up to the door, as Lucas made his way to her.

"Hi," she said, feeling embarrassed that so many eyes were on them.

Looking shocked, Lucas asked her, "How did you know where my parents live?"

"We didn't," Sofia answered. "We carol here every year and the lights have never been on." She pointed to the right, saying, "My brother's house is only two blocks away."

Smiling, because now he knew that there was truly Christmas magic, Lucas whispered, "And we

were never home before because we were with my
dad, out at the hospitals."

Crying now, Sofia looked up at him, her face
warm from his gaze. "You know, I wanted to wish
you a Merry Christmas and say that I love you."

Taking her hands into his, Lucas smirked.
"That's funny, because you see, I was going to find
you later and tell you exactly the same thing."

"Which part?" she asked. "Merry Christmas
or I love you?"

Kneeling down, Lucas said, "Both, of course."
He pulled out a ring that he had asked his mother
for earlier. It was a large diamond, surrounded
with rubies. She always said his father gave it to
her to remind her of Christmas.

Lucas peeked around Sofia, looking at the
crowd, and hollered, "I hope Sofia's father is here,
and he'll let me have his daughter's hand in
marriage!"

Neal Randall stepped forward, impressed that
the young man, whom he never met, had the
courage to ask. "Well, from what our
granddaughter told us, you're a good guy." He

looked back and smiled at his wife. "So, you have our permission."

Nodding, Lucas looked back up at Sofia. "I promise that I'll try to make every day as magical as Christmas for you, and I'll try really, really hard to learn to wrap my own presents."

The crowd laughed.

Looking down at this beautiful man, with his beautiful heart, Sofia couldn't think of a better person she could love. She answered, "Well, then I'll try to make every day as special as Christmas and I'll try really, really hard to shovel the driveway as good as you can."

"Kiss her already, boy!" William yelled from the front doorway of the house.

He looked over at Chelsea and winked, then put his finger to the side of his nose, just like Santa in Twas the Night Before Christmas.

Chelsea winked back, and waved. She knew Santa was the real deal, because he had given her aunt love.

On Christmas morning, everyone was gathered at Lucas's parents' house. It seemed easier to meet there, so William wouldn't have to travel. The night before, they agreed on a brunch there, to celebrate their two families, then dinner would be served at Sofia's house.

Everyone was chatting and laughing at the table, when Grant stood up. "I'd like to propose a toast," he lifted his glass of juice, "to Lucas and Sofia. May their life be filled with love."

"Here, here," Everyone answered and clinked glasses.

Clearing his throat, Grant kept standing, and added, "And, Nicole and I want to announce that we're expecting another baby."

There was silence for a full minute, and then the room erupted into congratulations and applause. Neal clapped his son on the back.

At the end of the table, Chelsea sat there, staring at her parents. Then she looked over at William, who nodded knowingly and winked. "This was the best Christmas wish ever!" she exclaimed. And William laughed.

Sometimes the things we wish for the hardest and longest, really do come true.

Merry Christmas!